THE BITEBACK DICTIONARY OF
HUMOROUS BUSINESS QUOTATIONS

The Biteback Dictionary of

HUMOROUS

BUSINESS

QUOTATIONS

—— *Fred Metcalf* ——

\B^b\

Biteback Publishing

First published in Great Britain in 2014 by
Biteback Publishing Ltd
Westminster Tower
3 Albert Embankment
London SE1 7SP
Copyright © Fred Metcalf 2014

ISBN 978-1-84954-227-2

10 9 8 7 6 5 4 3 2 1

A CIP catalogue record for this book is available from the British Library.

Set in Sabon and Neutra

Printed and bound in Great Britain by
CPI Group (UK) Ltd, Croydon CR0 4YY

CONTENTS

INTRODUCTION

Three volumes preceded this: the Biteback Dictionaries of Humorous Political Quotations, of Humorous Sporting Quotations and of Humorous Literary Quotations.

And now to Business.

My hope is that this is a book that both inspires and amuses. Within these laughter-laden pages you'll find, from Accountancy to Youth, hundreds of quotations, jokes, one-liners, epigrams, aphorisms, and adages. And advice. It's a book designed for close study, for light browsing and for, perhaps, providing the building blocks for first-class speech writing. I certainly hope that many of you dipping into this collection are doing so seeking a few 'well-chosen words' for a business speech. If so, you've come to the right book. So here's how to turn a seemingly innocent book of business quotations into an amusing, effective and thought-provoking speech machine.

SPEECH WRITING FOR BEGINNERS: YOUR QUESTIONS ANSWERED

For example: How important, actually, is a good speech?

Jenkin Lloyd Jones, the American newspaper publisher,

pointed out that 'A speech is a solemn responsibility. The man who makes a bad thirty-minute speech to two hundred people wastes only a half-hour of his own time. But he wastes 100 hours of the audience's time – more than four days – which should be a hanging offense.'

So no pressure there, then.

Next question: What should I expect from an audience?

Well, according to the American Vice-President Alben W. Barkley: 'The best audience is intelligent, well-educated and a little drunk.'

And, drunk or sober, how should I treat them?

'The great orator always shows a dash of contempt for the opinions of his audience,' said the American humorist Elbert Hubbard.

But how should I write the speech?

Firstly, think of a speech as a building. As well as a strong structure to hold it all together, you'll need a wealth of top-grade materials. Those materials? Jokes, quotes, anecdotes, statistics, facts and figures, personal stories and, of course, buckets of Aristotelian rhetorical devices. (More of those later. Much later. Certainly not in this volume!) And don't forget that it's OK to steal some of the materials. Within limits. As the English humorous writer Sally Poplin observed: 'All work and no plagiarism makes a dull speech.'

So how long should my speech be?

The English comic, Jerry Dennis provided this advice for speakers: 'If you don't know what to talk about, talk about three minutes.'

While the American comedian George Burns added, 'The secret of a good speech is to have a good beginning and a good ending and to keep the two as close together as possible.'

Muriel, the wife of American Vice-President Hubert Humphrey, offered this advice to her husband: 'Hubert, a speech does not need to be eternal to be immortal.'

Which reminds me of a remark from Senator Barry Goldwater on the subject of Hubert Humphrey and his speaking style: 'He talks so fast that listening to him is like trying to read *Playboy* magazine with your wife turning over the pages.'

OK, I'm ready. So how should I start the speech?

It's important to grab the audience's attention right from the top, perhaps with a startling statistic. Or try a joke. The intro should make the audience like you, and people like people who make them laugh.

So what sort of joke?

An apology for absence, for example, or a reference to the weather or to the meal you may have all just consumed.

A reference to the meal?

Right. Like this from the British politician David Mellor:

'I was just thinking, what a remarkable coincidence. Six hundred people eating here tonight – and we all ordered the same thing!'

A popular comedy device is to look up the day's date on Google as an inspiration for a joke.

For example?

This from DJ Kenny Everett: 'I see from my diary that it's 16 December. On this day ten years ago in Liverpool, a Chinese restaurant for dieters opened. They served all you could eat for 50p. Trouble is, they only gave you one chopstick!'

So, how long will it take me to write the speech?

It depends. Take this advice from the American President Woodrow Wilson: 'If I am to speak for ten minutes, I need a week for preparation; if fifteen minutes, three days; if half an hour, two days; if an hour, I am ready now.'

The American novelist Mark Twain added: 'It usually takes me more than three weeks to prepare a good impromptu speech.'

Anything else?

Yes. Read it out loud when you're writing it. And keep sentences short. Like this.

Speak like people – that means you – talk. Stay conversational.

So what if I'm invited to make an off-the cuff speech?

If it's at all possible, prepare! As the English wit Frederick Oliver said, 'Spontaneous speeches are seldom worth the paper they are not written on.'

Listen to the playwright George Bernard Shaw: 'I am the most spontaneous speaker in the world because every word, every gesture, and every retort has been carefully rehearsed.'

As President Richard Nixon said once in New York City: 'A good off-the-cuff, informal speech takes more preparation than a formal speech...'

So the advice is, steer clear of off-the-cuff unless you're *fully* prepared.

And in conclusion?

The British Conservative Lord Mancroft once said, 'A speech is like a love affair. Any fool can start it, but to end it requires considerable skill.'

The conclusion is important. You need to leave your

audience informed and entertained and with something to think about.

Any final thoughts?

Certainly. In public speaking, as in other fields of endeavour, the support of a top team – sharing the dream – is essential. I've been lucky enough to benefit from just such a first-class crew here at Biteback Publishing. Under widely respected team captain Iain Dale, I've been lucky enough to have on board Sam Carter, Hollie Teague, Namkwan Cho and Olivia Beattie.

I'd like to speak up for them all!

A

#ACCOUNTANCY

When you make the mistake of adding the date to the right side of the accounting statement, you must add it to the left side too.

Accountant's maxim

An accountant is a man hired to explain that you didn't make the money you did.

Anon.

An accountant is someone who tells you what to do with your money after you've done something else with it.

Anon.

I have no use for bodyguards, but I have a very special use for two highly trained certified public accountants.

Elvis Presley

An accountant is someone who solves a problem you didn't know you had in a way you don't understand.

Anon.

Our chief accountant is shy and retiring. He's half a million dollars shy, and that's why he's retiring.

Anon.

Never ask of money spent
Where the spender thinks it went.
Nobody was ever meant
To remember or invent
What he did with every cent.

Robert Frost, *The Hardship of Accounting* (1936)

My accountant called me. He said, 'I've got some terrible news for you. Last year was the best you've ever had.'

Max Kauffmann, American comedian

Companies run by engineers don't make any money, but companies run by accountants don't make anything at all.

Peter Krueger

If you are truly serious about preparing your child for the future, don't teach him to subtract – teach him to deduct.

Fran Lebowitz, New York columnist

There's no business like show business, but there are several businesses like accounting.

David Letterman, American television host

From Top Ten Things You Don't Want to Hear from your Accountant

- I'll gladly waive my fee for a night with your wife.
- Do you have any dedemptions or exuptions or whatever?
- Screw the computer – I do all my work on an Etch-A-Sketch.
- You can't claim yourself as your own spouse.

David Letterman, American television host

From Top Ten Reasons I Love Being an Accountant

- CPA training ensures I'm cool in high-pressure situations, like calculating the tip at Applebee's.
- While other poor losers go off to work in jeans and sneakers, I get to wear a suit.
- You haven't lived until you've filled out form 3277.
- What can I say – I'm an adrenaline junkie.
- Women don't expect much in the bedroom.

David Letterman, American television host

Our Accounting Department is the office that has the little red box on the wall saying, 'In case of emergency, please break glass.' And inside are two tickets to Brazil.

Robert Orben, American comedy writer

I've got an absolutely brilliant accountant. They've just named a loophole after him.

Sally Poplin, British humorous writer

… in your report here, it says that you are an extremely dull person. Our experts describe you as an appallingly dull fellow, unimaginative, timid, spineless, easily dominated, no sense of humour, tedious company and irrepressibly drab and awful.

And whereas in most professions these would be considered drawbacks, in accountancy they are a positive boon.

Monty Python, *And Now for Something Completely Different* (1971)

See also #FINANCE

#ADVERTISING

Advertisements contain the only truths to be relied on in a newspaper.

Thomas Jefferson, Founding Father and President of the United States, 1801–09

Advertising has annihilated the power of the most powerful adjectives.

Paul Valéry, French novelist and playwright

Advertising is what you do when you can't go to see somebody. That's all it is.

Fairfax Cone, veteran ad man

Few people at the beginning of the nineteenth century needed an ad man to tell them what they wanted.

John Kenneth Galbraith, Canadian economist

The spider looks for a merchant who doesn't advertise so he can spin a web across his door and lead a life of undisturbed peace.

Mark Twain, American author

Nothing except the mint can make money without advertising.

Thomas B. Macaulay, English author and historian

Advertising is a racket ... its constructive contribution to humanity is exactly minus zero.

F. Scott Fitzgerald, American author

Advertising is a valuable economic factor because it's the cheapest way of selling goods, especially if the goods are worthless.

Sinclair Lewis, American novelist and playwright

Advertising agency: 85 per cent confusion and 15 per cent commission.

Fred Allen, American comedian

The codfish lays ten thousand eggs,
The homely hen lays one.
The codfish never cackles
To tell you what she's done.
And so we scorn the codfish,
While the humble hen we prize,
Which only goes to show you
That it pays to advertise.

Anon., *It Pays to Advertise*

When the client moans and sighs
Make his logo twice the size.
If he still should prove refractory,
Show a picture of his factory.
Only in the gravest cases
Should you show the clients' faces.
    Anon.

The number of agency people required to shoot a commercial on location is in direct proportion to the mean temperature of the location.
    Anon.

In general, my children refused to eat anything that hadn't danced on TV.
    Erma Bombeck, American humorist

When a man throws an empty cigarette package from an automobile, he is liable to a fine of $50. When a man throws a billboard across a view, he is richly rewarded.
    Pat Brown, Governor of California 1959–67

The very first law in advertising is to avoid the concrete promise and cultivate the delightfully vague.
    Bill Cosby, American comedian and actor

The longest word in the English language is the one following the phrase: 'And now a word from our sponsor.'
    Hal Eaton, *Reader's Digest* (1949)

Everybody sat around thinking about Panasonic, the Japanese electronics account. Finally I decided, what the hell, I'll throw a line to loosen them up ... 'The headline is, the headline is: From Those Wonderful Folks Who Gave You Pearl Harbor.' Complete silence ...

Jerry Della Femina, *From Those Wonderful Folks Who Gave You Pearl Harbor* (1970)

Advertising – a judicious mixture of flattery and threats.

Northrop Frye, Canadian literary critic

Advertising is salesmanship mass produced.

Morris Hite, legendary American ad man

Doing business without advertising is like winking at a girl in the dark: you know what you are doing, but nobody else does.

Edgar Watson Howe, American writer

I do not read advertisements. I would spend all my time wanting things.

Franz Kafka, novelist

Advertising may be described as the science of arresting the human intelligence long enough to get money from it.

Stephen Leacock, Canadian humorist

Is it not clear that a product which must spend fortunes advertising, drawing attention to itself, is probably not one we need.

David Mamet, American playwright

I have ... had a disturbing dream in which I break through a cave wall near Nag Hammadi and discover urns full of ancient Coptic scrolls. As I unfurl the first scroll, a subscription card to some Gnostic exercise magazine flutters out.

    Colin McEnroe, American columnist and radio host

I saw a TV commercial that said, 'Kiss your haemorrhoids goodbye.'
Not even if I could.

    John Mendoza, American stand-up comedian

I think that I shall never see
A billboard lovely as a tree.
Indeed, unless the billboards fall
I'll never see a tree at all.

    Ogden Nash, 'Song of the Open Road' (1933)

In the ad biz, sincerity is a commodity bought and paid for like everything else.

    Newsweek (1967)

Advertising is the rattling of a stick inside a swill bucket.

    George Orwell, English writer

Advertising that uses superlatives isn't.

    Harry Pesin, *Sayings to Run an Advertising Agency By* (1966)

Fie on clients who cannot leave copy alone and fie on copywriters who can.

    Harry Pesin

I found something fascinating in the small ads today: FOR SALE Two single beds and a worn carpet.

Sally Poplin, British humorous writer

We've upped our standards!
Now up yours!

Radio station jingle (1998)

Creative people are like a wet towel. You wring them out and pick up another one.

Charles Revson, American cosmetics magnate

If advertisers spent the same amount of money improving their products as they do on advertising them, they wouldn't have to advertise them.

Will Rogers, American humorist

With the supermarket as our temple and the singing commercial as our litany, are we likely to fire the world with an irresistible vision of America's exalted purpose and inspiring way of life?

Adlai Stevenson, American politician

IF IT'S IN STOCK, WE HAVE IT!

Sign outside General Store, Iowa

Early to bed, early to rise, work like hell, and advertise.

Ted Turner, American broadcasting magnate

Pretend you're in a perfume advert by saying words that bear no relevance to each other while riding a diamanté stallion up your own arse.

Twitter, 2012

The only reason I made a commercial for American Express was to pay for my American Express bill.

Peter Ustinov, English actor and writer

See also #MARKETING, #SLOGANS

#ADVICE

Aim low, reach your goals, and avoid disappointment.

Scott Adams, American cartoonist and creator of *Dilbert*

There is nothing we receive with so much reluctance as advice.

Joseph Addison, English writer

Never put off until tomorrow what you can avoid altogether.

Anon.

If everything seems to be coming your way, you're probably in the wrong lane.

Anon.

Advice: the suggestions you give someone else which you hope will work to your benefit.

Ambrose Bierce, *The Devil's Dictionary* (1911)

I owe my success to having listened respectfully to the very best advice and then going away and doing the exact opposite.

G. K. Chesterton, English writer

In those days he was wiser than he is now; he used to frequently take my advice.

Winston Churchill, British statesman and orator

It's never too late to be what you might have been.

George Eliot, English novelist

Start off every day with a smile and get it over with.

W. C. Fields, American actor and comedian

The best advice I've ever received is 'No one else knows what they're doing either.'

Ricky Gervais, English comedian

When you counsel someone, you should appear to be reminding him of something he had forgotten, not of the light he was unable to see.

Baltasar Gracián, Spanish philosopher

A never failing way to get rid of a fellow is to tell him something for his own good.

Kin Hubbard, American cartoonist

Of the few innocent pleasures left to men past middle life, the jamming of common sense down the throats of fools is perhaps the keenest.

T. H. Huxley, English biologist

Advice is what we ask for when we already know the answer but wish we didn't.

Erica Jong, American novelist

Never pick up someone else's ringing telephone.

Mark McCormack, founder and chairman of IMG

Most of us would rather risk a catastrophe than read the instructions.

Mignon McLaughlin, American journalist

Fourteen Things You Really Ought to Know by Now:
1. When a person with experience meets a person with money, the person with experience will get the money. And the person with the money will get the experience.
2. If you can smile when things go wrong, you have someone in mind to blame.
3. The facts, although interesting, are irrelevant.
4. Anything worth fighting for is worth fighting dirty for.
5. Friends may come and friends may go, but enemies accumulate.
6. If you think there is good in everybody, you haven't met everybody.
7. There is always one more imbecile than you counted on.
8. Money isn't everything. In fact, most of the time it isn't even enough.
9. If you work hard eight hours a day, you can become the boss and work *sixteen* hours a day.
10. A big shot is a little shot who kept shooting.
11. Artificial Intelligence is no match for Natural Stupidity.
12. If at first you don't succeed – try management.

13. Never underestimate the power of very stupid people in large groups.
14. Go the extra mile – It makes your boss look like an incompetent slacker.
     Sally Poplin, British humorous writer

We are so happy to advise others that occasionally we even do it in their interest.
     Jules Renard, French author

Speak softly and carry a big stick; you will go far.
     Theodore Roosevelt, President of the United States
     1901–09

Never invest in anything that eats or needs repairing.
     Billy Rose, American showman and impresario

No one wants advice, only corroboration.
     John Steinbeck, American novelist

The art of advice is to make the recipient believe he thought of it himself.
     Frank Tyger, American cartoonist and columnist

There is no human problem which could not be solved if people would simply do as I advise.
     Gore Vidal, American writer and political commentator

See also #APHORISMS, #CONSULTANTS, #WORDS OF WISDOM

#AMBITION

I Want It All – And I Want It Delivered!
  Anon.

[John Patten MP] … is so ambitious that he squeaks when he walks, and cannot manage to smile at any colleague inferior in rank in case he compromises himself in some way.
  Alan Clark, British politician

Never keep up with the Joneses. Drag them down to your level; it's cheaper.
  Quentin Crisp, English writer and raconteur

Less than perfect financial circumstances are the keenest spur to further endeavour.
  Joe Davis, British sportsman

I want to be what I was when I wanted to be what I am now.
  Jerry Dennis, British comedian

Ambition is most aroused by the trumpet-clang of another's fame.
  Baltasar Gracián, Spanish philosopher

What is my loftiest ambition? I've always wanted to throw an egg into an electric fan.
  Oliver Herford, American artist and writer

Nothing is so commonplace as to wish to be remarkable.
  Oliver Wendell Holmes, American physician and poet

Every morning I get up and look through the *Forbes* list of the Richest People in America. And if I'm not there, I go to work.

Robert Orben, American comedy writer

People say follow your dreams.
So I went back to sleep.

Pinterest, 2013

I always wanted to be somebody; but I should have been more specific.

Lily Tomlin, American comedian

Ambition is the last refuge of the failure.

Oscar Wilde, *Phrases and Philosophies for the Use of the Young* (1894)

I intend to live forever. So far, so good.

Steven Wright, American comedian

We're supposed to be perfect our first day on the job, and then show constant improvement.

Ed Vargo, baseball umpire

The only way to accept an insult is to ignore it. If you can't ignore it, top it. If you can't top it, laugh at it. If you can't laugh at it, it's probably deserved.

Joseph Russell Lynes, Jr, American author and editor

See also #GOALS

#APHORISMS

Today is the first day of the rest of your life, but so was yesterday, and look how that turned out...
    Facebook, 2010

It ain't bragging if you can do it!
    Babe Ruth, American baseball player

Always forgive your enemies. Nothing annoys them more.
    Oscar Wilde, Irish playwright

Failure is not an option – it comes bundled with the software.
    Anon.

A picture is worth 1,000 words, but it uses up 3,000 times more memory.
    Anon.

Eagles soar, but weasels don't get sucked into jet engines.
    Anon.

Music hath charms to soothe the savage beast – but I'd try a revolver first.
    Josh Billings, American wit

See also #WORDS OF WISDOM

B

#BANKRUPTCY

Capitalism without bankruptcy is like Christianity without hell.

Frank Borman, NASA astronaut

He certainly had a lot of nerve. He took a taxi to the bankruptcy court, and invited the driver in as a creditor!

Jerry Dennis, British comedian

My friend was facing bankruptcy. In his despair, he turned to the Bible for consolation – and opened it at Chapter 11.

Max Kauffmann, American comedian

See also #BORROWING AND LENDING, #DEBT

#BANKS AND BANKING

I had a hard time at the bank today. I tried to take out a loan but they turned me down. Apparently they won't accept the voices in my head as references.

Steve Altman, American comedian

A banker is a man who lends you an umbrella when the weather is fair, and takes it away from you when it rains.

Anon.

… [Bankers] all observe one rule which woe betides the banker who fails to heed it,
Which is you must never lend any money to anybody unless they don't need it.

Ogden Nash, 'Bankers are Just Like Anybody Else, except Richer' (1938)

A lot of people will also urge you to put some money in a bank, and in fact within reason – this is very good advice. But don't go overboard. Remember, what you are doing is giving your money to somebody else to hold on to, and I think that it is worth keeping in mind that the businessmen who run banks are so worried about holding on to things that they put little chains on all their pens.

Miss Piggy, *Miss Piggy's Guide to Life (As Told to Henry Beard)* (1981) There have been three great inventions since the beginning of time: fire, the wheel and central banking.

Will Rogers, American humorist

If you owe the bank $100, that's your problem. If you owe the bank $100 million, that's the bank's problem.

J. Paul Getty, American industrialist

A bank is a financial institution from which you can borrow money as long as you can provide sufficient evidence to show you don't need it.

Sally Poplin, British humorous writer

It is easier to rob by setting up a bank than by holding up a bank clerk.

Bertolt Brecht, German poet and playwright

I don't trust banks to get their figures right. If bankers can count, why do they always have six windows and two cashiers?

Anon.

Over a long weekend, I could teach my dog to be an investment banker.

Herbert A. Allen, American businessman and stockbroker

Banking may well be a career from which no man really recovers.

John Kenneth Galbraith, Canadian economist

Gentlemen, you are as fine a group of men as ever foreclosed a mortgage on a widow. I'm glad to be among you shylocks.

Will Rogers, American humorist

See also #FINANCE

#BIG BUSINESS AND CORPORATIONS

Coca-Cola Co. discovered that it had inadvertently bought Columbia Pictures Inc. Company executives had thought they were buying Columbia, the Central America country. Coca-Cola is asking the movie company for its deposit back.

Off The Wall Street Journal (1982)

IBM is making top corporate positions hereditary. The sweeping change is designed to take advantage of new estate tax laws and stimulate child production among the right people.

Off The Wall Street Journal (1982)

The meek may inherit the earth – but not its mineral rights.

J. Paul Getty, American industrialist

If the government was as afraid of disturbing the consumer as it is of disturbing business, this would be some democracy.

Kin Hubbard, American cartoonist

If you believe that ten guys in pin-striped suits are back in kindergarten class playing with building blocks, you will get a rough picture of what life in a corporation is like.

Lee Iacocca, American businessman

Whenever you're sitting across from some important person, always picture him sitting there in a suit of long red underwear. That's the way I always operated in business.

Joseph P. Kennedy II, American politician

Nothing is illegal if a hundred businessmen decide to do it, and that's true anywhere in the world.

Andrew Young, American diplomat

Corporation: an ingenious device for obtaining individual profit without individual responsibility.

Ambrose Bierce, *The Devil's Dictionary* (1911)

A corporation cannot blush.

Howell Walsh, American lawyer

Too many people are on boards because they want to have nice-looking visiting cards.

Utz Felcht, German businessman

There is nothing more short-term than a sixty-year-old CEO holding a fistful of share options.

Gary Hamel, American businessman and writer

In a company of 2,500 people, there are 2,500 egos running around, each with his or her view of reality.

Mark McCormack, American founder and chairman of IMG

I come from an environment where, if you see a snake, you kill it. At General Motors, if you see a snake, the first thing you do is hire a consultant on snakes.

H. Ross Perot, American entrepreneur and politician

I believe in God, family and McDonald's. And, in the office, that order is reversed.

Ray Kroc, founder of the Ronald McDonald Foundation

If you're not scared, you're too stupid to work here.

Lee Iacocca, American businessman

Synergy, the most screwball buzzword of the past decade.

Harold S. Geneen, *The Synergy Myth* (1997)

Lethargy bordering on sloth remains the cornerstone of our investment style.

Warren Buffett, American entrepreneur and financier

[Gallup:] A for-profit think tank...

Jim Clifton, CEO of Gallup

In the insurance business there is no statute of limitations on stupidity.

Warren Buffett, American entrepreneur and financier

We don't care. We don't have to. We're the phone company.

Ernestine the phone operator, *Laugh-In*

#BORROWING AND LENDING

The human species, according to the best theory I can form of it, is composed of two distinct races, the men who borrow and the men who lend.

Charles Lamb, English essayist

There is no point in borrowing if you mean to pay it back.

Anon.

I need enough to tide me over till I need more.

Bill Hoest, American cartoonist

Always borrow money from a pessimist; he doesn't expect to be paid back.

Anon.

If you lend someone $20, and never see that person again, it was probably worth it.

Anon.

See also #BANKRUPTCY, #BANKS AND BANKING, #DEBT

#BOSSES

Show me an orchestra that likes its conductor and I'll show you a lousy conductor.

Goddard Lieberson, President of Columbia Records

An executive is someone who can take three hours for lunch without hindering production.

Anon.

Do not underestimate your abilities. That is your boss's job.

Anon.

Never work for a boss who opens the company mail.

Anon.

If you think your boss is stupid, remember: you wouldn't have a job if he was any smarter.

Albert A. Grant, American wit

We are CEO's of our own companies, Me Inc. To be in business today, our most important job is to be head marketer for the brand called 'You'.

Tom Peters, business guru

You always knew where you stood with Sam Goldwyn: nowhere.

F. Scott Fitzgerald, American novelist

A boss is a person who's in early when you're late and in late when you're early.

Sally Poplin, British humorous writer

His secretary tells me that Jim is one of those very special bosses who believe in sharing the credit with the person who actually did the work.

Anon.

If this company appoints any more executives, there'll be nobody left to do the work.

Anon.

You can't help liking the managing director – if you don't, he fires you.

Anon.

Two things to help keep one's job. First, let the boss think he's having his own way. Second, let him have it.

Sam Ewing, American author

Top Boss Lines by Jerry Dennis

- A boss is someone who delegates all the authority, shifts all the blame and takes all the credit.
- He was the most hated man in the company. Every time he called a staff meeting, it started with a strip-search.
- I told my boss that I went to church and prayed for a raise. He told me never to go over his head again!
- I've got a very flexible boss. He lets me come in any time I want before nine and leave any time I want after five.
- My boss is so mean, if you get in two minutes late he fines you and if you get in two minutes early he charges you rent.
- Oh, so you're Jim's boss! He's always mentioning your name, Mr Slavedriver!
- OK, you can have the job as my assistant. But I don't just want a yes-man. Agreed?
- Please understand, this is just a suggestion. You don't have to do it unless you want to keep your job.

You think it's easy being a boss? Every day I have to get up early to see who comes into work late!

Max Kauffmann, American comedian

I don't want any yes-men around me. I want everybody to tell me the truth even if it costs them their jobs.

Samuel Goldwyn, Hollywood producer

See also #LEADERSHIP, #MANAGEMENT

#BUDGETS

There are several ways in which to apportion the family income, all of them unsatisfactory.

Robert Benchley, American wit

Some couples go over their budgets very carefully every month, others just go over them.

Sally Poplin, British humorous writer

All decent people live beyond their incomes nowadays, and those who aren't respectable live beyond other people's. A few gifted individuals manage to do both.

Saki (H. H. Munro), *The Matchmaker* (1911)

Solvency is entirely a matter of temperament and not of income.

Logan Pearsall Smith, *Afterthoughts* (1931)

Anyone who lives within his means suffers from a lack of imagination.

Oscar Wilde, Irish playwright

Just about the time you think you can make both ends meet, somebody moves the ends.

Pansy Penner, American writer

I gave him an unlimited budget – and he exceeded it.

Edward Bennett Williams, American lawyer and former owner of Washington Redskins American football club, of his former head coach George Allen

Why is there so much month left at the end of the money?
  Anon.

My problem lies in reconciling my gross habits with my net income.
  Errol Flynn, Hollywood actor and hell-raiser

I would rather have my people laugh at my economies than weep for my extravagance.
  Oscar II, King of Norway and Sweden

See also #ACCOUNTANCY, #MONEY

#BUREAUCRACY

These are the guidelines for bureaucrats:
1. When in charge, ponder.
2. When in trouble, delegate.
3. When in doubt, mumble.
  James H. Boren, American humorist

The man who is denied the opportunity of taking decisions of importance begins to regard as important the decisions he is allowed to take. He becomes fussy about filing, keen on seeing pencils are sharpened, eager to ensure that windows are opened (or shut) and apt to use two or three different coloured pencils.
  C. Northcote Parkinson, British naval historian and author

Some civil servants are neither servants nor civil.

Winston Churchill, British statesman and orator

What the world really needs is more love and less paperwork.

Pearl Bailey, American singer

If there's anything a public servant hates to do, it's something for the public.

Kin Hubbard, American cartoonist

There is something about a bureaucrat that does not like a poem.

Gore Vidal, American writer and political commentator

The only thing that saves us from the bureaucracy is its inefficiency.

Eugene McCarthy, American politician

If you don't know what to do with many of the papers piled on your desk, stick a dozen colleagues' initials on them and pass them along. When in doubt, route.

Malcolm S. Forbes, American publisher

Bureaucracy is a giant mechanism operated by pygmies.

Honoré de Balzac, French writer

#BUSINESS

Business has been described as the art of extracting money from another man's pocket without resort to violence.

Anon.

The businessman – the man to whom age brings golf instead of wisdom.

George Bernard Shaw, Irish playwright

Commerce, that pride and darling of our ocean, that educator of nations, that benefactor in spite of itself.

Ralph Waldo Emerson, American essayist and poet

It took me years to work out the difference between net and gross. In meetings I just used to say, 'Tell me if it's good or bad news.'

Richard Branson, British business magnate

Business is like sex. When it's good, it's very, very good, when it's not so good, it's still good.

George Katona, American psychologist and economist

Commerce is the equaliser of the wealth of nations.

William Gladstone, four-time British Prime Minister

It is not the employer who pays the wages – he only handles the money. It's the product that pays the wages.

Henry Ford, American industrialist

A businessman is a hybrid of a dancer and a calculator.

Paul Valéry, French novelist and playwright

To sell something you have to someone who wants it – that is not business.

But to sell something you don't have to someone who doesn't want it – that's business.

　　Anon.

Most of my contemporaries at school entered the World of Business, the logical destiny of bores.

　　Barry Humphries, Australian wit

We're a non-profit-making organisation. We don't mean to be, but we are.

　　Jerry Dennis, British comedian

How do you make money selling your watches so cheaply? Easy. We make a fortune repairing them.

　　Anon.

The great thing about being in business for yourself is that you get to make all the big decisions.

Like will you work fourteen hours today or just twelve?

Seven days this week or just six?

Will you develop an ulcer or just collapse from exhaustion?

　　Anon.

The directors decided to award an annual prize of fifty pounds for the best idea for saving the company money. It was won by a young executive who suggested that in future the prize money be reduced to ten pounds.

　　Anon.

Business is what, when you don't have any, you get out of.
  Sally Poplin, British humorous writer

Chairman: Right, let's vote on the recommendation. All those against, raise their hands and say, 'I resign.'
  Anon.

He's the world's worst businessman. If he was a florist, he'd close on Mother's Day.
  Anon.

I started this business on a shoestring and after six months I'd tripled my investment. Now I just want to know what to do with the spare shoestring.
  Anon.

The genius in industry is building things to last twenty years and making them obsolete in two.
  Anon.

Fools rush in where wise men fear to trade.
  Peter Drucker, American businessman and author

Business, someone said, is like riding a bicycle. Either you keep moving or you fall down.
  Sally Poplin, British humorous writer

Commerce is a plant that grows wherever there is peace, as soon as there is peace and as long as there is peace.
  Ralph Waldo Emerson, American essayist and poet

A great society is a society in which men of business think
greatly of their functions.

   Alfred North Whitehead, English mathematician and
   philosopher

He [the businessman] is the only man who is for ever apolo-
gizing for his occupation.

   H. L. Mencken, American journalist

See also #BIG BUSINESS AND CORPORATIONS

C

#CAPITALISM

Free enterprise will work if you will.
> Ray Kroc, founder of the Ronald McDonald Foundation

The trouble with the profit system has always been that it was highly unprofitable to most people.
> E. B. White, *One Man's Meat* (1944)

The inherent vice of capitalism is the unequal sharing of blessings; the inherent virtue of socialism is the equal sharing of miseries.
> Winston Churchill, British statesman and orator

Isn't capitalism wonderful! Under what other system could the ordinary man in the street owe so much?
> Sally Poplin, British humorous writer

Under capitalism, it's dog eat dog. Under Communism, it's just the opposite.
> Anon.

The fundamentals of capitalist ethics require that 'you shall earn your bread in sweat' – unless you happen to have private means.

Michal Kalecki, Polish economist

Capitalism works better than it sounds, while socialism sounds better than it works.

Richard Nixon, *Beyond Peace* (1994)

See also #COMPETITION, #SOCIALISM

#CHANGE

Change is inevitable, except from a vending machine.

Anon.

If you want to make enemies, try to change something.

Woodrow Wilson, President of the United States 1913–21

Most of the change we think we see in life is due to truths being in and out of favour.

Robert Frost, *The Black Cottage* (1914)

If it ain't broke, break it.

Richard Pascale, American management guru

Why does every generation have to think that it lives in the period with the greatest turbulence?

Henry Mintzberg, Canadian management guru

#COMMERCE

Someone has suggested that America's greatest gifts to civilisation are three: cornflakes, Kleenex and credit.
Louis T. Benezet, American educator

No nation was ever ruined by trade.
Benjamin Franklin, polymath and Founding Father of the United States

In matters of commerce, the fault of the Dutch
Is offering too little and asking too much.
The French are with equal advantage content
So we clap on Dutch bottoms just 20 per cent.
George Canning, British politician

What recommends commerce to me is its enterprise and bravery. It does not clasp its hands and pray to Jupiter.
Henry David Thoreau, American historian and philosopher

Do the Chinese realise that when they visit America, they buy souvenirs made in their own country?
Facebook, 2013

Commerce is the great civiliser. We exchange ideas when we exchange fabrics.
Robert Green Ingersoll, American lawyer

Buying and selling is good and necessary; it is very necessary, and may possibly be very good, but it cannot be the noblest work of man; and let us hope that in our time it may not be esteemed the noblest work of an Englishman.

Anthony Trollope, English novelist

The musician, the painter, the poet are, in a larger sense, no greater artists than the man of commerce.

W. S. Maverick, American wit

#COMMITTEES

A group that takes minutes and wastes hours.

Anon.

A group of the unfit appointed by the unwilling to do the unnecessary.

Carl C. Byers, American philosopher (attrib.)

We always carry out by committee anything in which any of us alone would be too reasonable to persist.

Frank Moore Colby, American educator and writer

Nothing is ever accomplished by committee unless it consists of three members, one of whom happens to be sick and the other absent.

Hendrik van Loon, American author and historian

Committee work is like a soft chair – easy to get into but hard to get out of.

Anon.

A committee is a thing which takes a week to do what one good man can do in an hour.

Elbert Hubbard, American writer

A committee is a cul-de-sac down which ideas are lured and then quietly strangled.

Barnett Cocks, Clerk of the House of Commons 1962–74

If Columbus had had an advisory committee he would probably still be at the dock.

Arthur Goldberg, American statesman and jurist

If you live in a country run by committee, be on the committee.

Anon.

Chapman's Rules for Serving on Committees
1. Never arrive on time; this stamps you as a beginner.
2. Don't say anything until the meeting is half over; this stamps you as being wise.
3. Be as vague as possible; this avoids irritating the others.
4. When in doubt, suggest that a subcommittee be appointed.
5. Be the first one to move for adjournment; this will make you popular; it's what everyone is waiting for.

Harry Chapman, *The Greater Kansas City Medical Bulletin* (1963)

#COMPETITION

I don't meet competition; I crush it.
   Charles Revson, American cosmetics magnate

Competition brings out the best in products and the worst
in people.
   David Sarnoff, American businessman and pioneer of radio

Thou shalt not covet, but tradition
Approves all forms of competition.
   Arthur Hugh Clough, 'The Latest Decalogue' (1862)

In a garage somewhere, an entrepreneur is forging a bullet
with your company's name on it.
   Gary Hamel, American businessman and writer

I feel sorry for those who live without competition ... Fat,
dumb and unhappy in cradle-to-grave security.
   Donald M. Kendall, CEO of PepsiCo

We're eyeball to eyeball and I think the other fellow just
blinked.
   Dean Rusk, American politician

See also #CAPITALISM

#COMPUTER PROGRAMMING

... then it occurred to me that a computer is a stupid machine with the ability to do incredibly smart things, while computer programmers are smart people with the ability to do incredibly stupid things. They are, in short, a perfect match.

Bill Bryson, American travel writer

The purpose of most computer languages is to lengthen your résumé by a word and a comma.

Larry Wall, computer programmer and author

[On debugging:] Another effective technique is to explain your code to someone else. This will often cause you to explain the bug to yourself. Sometimes it takes no more than a few sentences, followed by an embarrassed 'Never mind, I see what's wrong. Sorry to bother you.' This works remarkably well; you can even use non-programmers as listeners. One university computer centre kept a teddy bear near the help desk. Students with mysterious bugs were required to explain them to the bear before they could speak to a human counsellor.

Brian Kernighan and Rob Pike, computer experts

Programming is like sex. One mistake and you have to support it for the rest of your life.

Michael Sinz, systems architect

Always code as if the guy who ends up maintaining your code will be a violent psychopath who knows where you live.

Martin Golding, celebrated programmer

One man's crappy software is another man's full-time job.

Jessica Gaston, GMX Girl spokesmodel

We have come through a strange cycle in programming, starting with the creation of programming itself as a human activity. Executives with the tiniest smattering of knowledge assume that anyone can write a program, and only now are programmers beginning to win their battle for recognition as true professionals. Not just anyone, with any background, or any training, can do a fine job of programming. Programmers know this, but then why is it that they think that anyone picked off the street can do documentation? One has only to spend an hour looking at papers written by graduate students to realize the extent to which the ability to communicate is not universally held. And so, when we speak about computer program documentation, we are not speaking about the psychology of computer programming at all – except insofar as programmers have the illusion that anyone can do a good job of documentation, provided he is not smart enough to be a programmer.

Gerald Weinberg, American computer scientist

C makes it easy to shoot yourself in the foot; C++ makes it harder, but when you do, it blows away your whole leg.

Bjarne Stroustrup, Danish computer scientist

UNIX was not designed to stop its users from doing stupid things, as that would also stop them from doing clever things.

Doug Gwyn, UNIX expert

UNIX never says please.

Rob Pike, Canadian software engineer and author

When in doubt, use brute force.

Ken Thompson, computer science pioneer

Life is too short to run proprietary software.

Bdale Garbee, computer specialist

Mathematicians stand on each other's shoulders and computer scientists stand on each other's toes.

Richard Hamming, American mathematician and computer scientist

Crap can work. Given enough thrust pigs will fly, but it's not necessarily a good idea.

James Simmons, computer expert

Measuring programming progress by lines of code is like measuring aircraft building progress by weight.

Bill Gates, co-founder of Microsoft

Most software today is very much like an Egyptian pyramid with millions of bricks piled on top of each other, with no structural integrity, but just done by brute force and thousands of slaves.

Alan Kay, American computer scientist

If builders built buildings the way programmers wrote programs, then the first woodpecker that came along would destroy civilization.

Gerald Weinberg, American computer scientist

Sometimes it pays to stay in bed on Monday, rather than spending the rest of the week debugging Monday's code.

Dan Salomon, programmer

I really hate this damn machine;
I wish that they would sell it.
It won't do what I want it to,
But only what I tell it.

Anon.

Beta. Software undergoes beta testing shortly before it's released. Beta is Latin for 'still doesn't work'.

Anon.

Version 1 of any software is full of bugs. Version 2 fixes all the bugs and is great. Version 3 adds all the things users ask for, but hides all the great stuff in Version 2.

Fred Blechman, American author

Great software, likewise, requires a fanatical devotion to beauty. If you look inside good software, you find that parts no one is ever supposed to see are beautiful too. I'm not claiming I write great software, but I know that when it comes to code I behave in a way that would make me eligible for prescription drugs if I approached everyday life the same way. It drives me crazy to see code that's badly indented, or that uses ugly variable names.

Paul Graham, *Hackers and Painters* (2003)

Programming today is a race between software engineers striving to build bigger and better idiot-proof programs, and the Universe trying to produce bigger and better idiots. So far, the Universe is winning.

Rich Cook, academic and programmer

Program, *n*. A magic spell cast over a computer allowing it to turn one's input into error messages; v. tr. To engage in a pastime similar to banging one's head against a wall, but with fewer opportunities for reward.

Anon.

There are two ways to write error-free programs; only the third one works.

Alan J. Perlis, American computer scientist

See also #COMPUTERS

#COMPUTERS

Bill Gates is a very rich man today ... and do you want to know why? The answer is one word: versions.

Dave Barry, American author and columnist

Name your kids 'Control', 'Alt', and 'Delete' so when they fuck up you can just hit them all at once.
Anon.

My office password's been hacked. That's the third time I've had to rename the cat.
Twitter, 2013

If at first you don't succeed, call it *Version 1.0*.
Anon.

My computer dating came up with a perfect gentleman. Still, I've got another three goes.
Sally Poplin, British humorous writer

All power tends to corrupt. PowerPoint corrupts absolutely.
Ed Tufte, *Wired* magazine

Abandon all hope, you who press ENTER here.
Anon.

To err is human, but to really foul things up requires a computer.
Anon.

If a packet hits a pocket on a socket on a port,
And the bus is interrupted as a very last resort,
And the address of the memory makes your floppy disk abort,
Then the socket packet pocket has an error to report.
If your cursor finds a menu item followed by a dash,
And the double-clicking icon puts your window in the trash,

And your data is corrupted 'cos the index doesn't hash,
Then your situation's hopeless and your system's gonna crash!
If the label on the cable on the table in your house
Says the network is connected to the button on your mouse,
But your packets want to tunnel on another protocol
That's repeatedly rejected by the printer down the hall,
And your screen is all distorted by the side-effects of gauss,
So your icons in the window are as wavy as a souse,
Then you may as well reboot and go out with a bang,
'Cos as sure as I'm a poet, the sucker's gonna hang!
When the copy of your floppy's getting sloppy on the disk,
And the macro-code instructions cause unnecessary risk,
Then you'll have to flash your memory and you'll want to
    RAM your ROM.
Quickly turn off your computer and be sure to tell
    your mom.
    Anon., *Dr Seuss Explains Computers*

Doonesbury: Excuse me, sir. Do you have any user-friendly
sales reps?
Store manager: You mean consumer-compatible liveware?
No, he's off today.
    Garry Trudeau, American cartoonist

Five Rules of the Computer:
1. There's never time to do it right, but always time to do
   it again.
2. Inside every large program is a small program trying to
   get out.
3. It's morally wrong to allow naive end-users to keep their
   money.

4. Never test for errors you can't handle.
5. If you think the problems is bad now, just wait until we've solved it.

Anon.

Ten Computer One-Liners by Jerry Dennis

1. Computers aren't intelligent. They only think they are.
2. As a computer, I find your faith in technology amusing.
3. Windows – just another pane in the glass.
4. Press CTRL-ALT-DEL to continue
5. My new computer printer can produce 200 pages a minute. It certainly cuts down on the paperwork!
6. In the US government's fight with Bill Gates, I'm for the government. I always like to root for the little guy.
7. The computer is a great invention. There are as many mistakes as ever but now it's nobody's fault.
8. They sacked a guy at the office because they found a computer that could do everything he could do. Sadly, when he told his wife, she went out and bought the same computer.
9. They've invented the perfect computer. If it makes a mistake it blames another computer!
10. They say that computers can't think, but I have one that does. It thinks it's broken.

Boss: Why is it that every time I come into your office, you're playing video games on your computer?
Programmer: It must be that the carpeting in the hall muffles your footsteps.

Anon.

This computer will cut your workload by 50 per cent.
I'll take two of them!

Anon.

I'm old enough to remember the time when windows were what you shut when it was cold outside, a keyboard was where you hung your keys, modem was what you did to fields of hay – and, if you had a three-and-a-half-inch floppy, it was something you kept very quiet about.

Fred Metcalf, joke writer

If you put tomfoolery into a computer, nothing comes out but tomfoolery. But this tomfoolery, having passed through a very expensive machine, is somehow ennobled and no one dares criticise it.

Pierre Marie Gallois, French author

Five Reasons Why Computers Must Be Male

1. They're heavily dependent on external tools and equipment.
2. They'll usually do what you ask them to do, but they won't do more than they have to and they won't think of it on their own.
3. They periodically cut you off right when you think you've established a connection.
4. They're typically obsolete within five years and need to be traded in for a new model. Some users, however, feel that they've already invested so much in the machine that they're compelled to remain with an underpowered system.

5. They get hot when you turn them on and that's the only time you have their attention.
Anon.

Five Reasons Why Computers Must Be Female
1. No one but their creator understands their internal logic.
2. The native language used to communicate with other computers is incomprehensible to everyone else.
3. Even your smallest mistakes are immediately committed to memory for future reference.
4. The message 'Bad Command or Filename' is about as informative as 'If you don't know why I'm mad at you, then I'm certainly not going to tell you.'
5. As soon as you make a commitment to one, you find yourself spending half your salary on accessories for it.
Anon.

How to Tell if You're a Geek
• You tend to save the power leads from broken appliances.
• You own one or more white short-sleeved shirts.
• You have used coat hangers and duct tape for something other than hanging coats and taping ducts.
• You know what 'http' stands for.
• You own a slide rule and you know how to use it.
• Your wife sends you an email to call you to dinner.
• You once took the back off your TV just to see what's inside.
• Your laptop computer cost more than your car.
• You have more friends on the internet than in real life.
• You've tried to repair a five pound radio.

- You spend half of a plane trip with your laptop on your lap – and your child in the overhead compartment.
  Anon.

Fifteen Oxymorons:
1. Pretty ugly
2. Act naturally
3. Advanced BASIC
4. Genuine imitation
5. Good grief
6. Working holiday
7. Almost exactly
8. Government organisation
9. Alone together
10. Business ethics
11. Military intelligence
12. Peace force
13. Charm offensive
14. Fun run
15. Microsoft Works
    Anon.

Computers are like dogs. They smell fear.
   Simone Alexander, comedian

Announcing the new Built-in Orderly Organised Knowledge device: BOOK.
The BOOK is a revolutionary breakthrough in technology: no wires, no batteries, nothing to be connected or switched on. It's so easy to use even a child can operate it. Just lift its cover. Compact and portable, it can be used anywhere,

yet it is powerful enough to hold as much information as a CD-ROM disc. Each BOOK is constructed of sequentially numbered sheets of paper, each capable of holding thousands of bits of information. Each sheet is scanned optically, registering information directly into your brain. A flick of the finger takes you to the next sheet. The BOOK never crashes and never needs re-booting. The 'browse' feature allows you to move instantly to any sheet. Many come with an 'index' feature, which pinpoints the exact location of any selected information for instant retrieval.

An optional 'BOOKmark' accessory allows you to open the BOOK to the exact place you left it in a previous session. The BOOK is ideal for long-term archive use. Several field trials have proved that the medium will still be readable in several centuries' time.

You can also make personal notes next to BOOK text entries with an optional programming tool, the Portable Erasable Nib Cryptic Intercommunication Language Stylus (PENCILS). The BOOK's appeal seems so certain that thousands of content creators have committed to the platform.

Anon.

Q: How many Bill Gateses does it take to change a light bulb?
A: None. He calls a meeting and makes darkness the standard.

Anon.

Q: How many Microsoft tech-support people does it take to change a light bulb?
A: Please continue to hold. Your call is very important to us.
Anon.

Error Messages
- 'Bad Command or File Name. Good try, though.'
- 'Earth is 98 per cent full. Please delete anyone you can.'
- 'Enter any 11-digit prime number to continue …'
- 'Hit any user to continue.'
- 'Press any key … no, no, no, NOT THAT ONE!'
- 'Smash Forehead on Keyboard to Continue.'

   Anon.

Eye halve a spelling checker
It came with my Pea Sea,
It plane lee marks four my revue
Miss steaks aye dew knot sea.
Eye ran this poem threw it,
Your sure reel glad two no.
Its vary polished in its weigh
My checker tolled me sew …
… Sow ewe can sea why aye dew prays
Such soft wear four pea seas,
And why eye brake in two averse
Buy righting want too pleas.

   Mark Eckman and Jerrold H. Zar, 'An Owed Two The
   Spelling Checker'

It's not a bug, it's a feature!

   Anon.

SOFTWARE: These are the PROGRAMS that you put
on the HARD DRIVE by sticking them through the little
SLOT. The function of the software is to give instructions to
the CPU, which is a set of three initials inside the computer

that rapidly processes billions of tiny facts, called BYTES, and within a fraction of a second sends you an ERROR MESSAGE that requires you to call the CUSTOMER SUPPORT HOTLINE and be placed on HOLD for approximately the life span of a CARIBOU.

Dave Barry, *Dave Barry in Cyberspace* (1996)

Incompatible operating systems have taken over where religious differences left off.

Cathy Guisewite, American cartoonist and creator of *Cathy*

We used to have lots of questions to which there were no answers. Now, with the computer there are lots of answers to which we haven't thought up the questions.

Peter Ustinov, English actor and writer

When I'm around hard-core computer geeks, I wanna say, 'Come outside, the graphics are great!'

Matt Weinhold, American comic

Home computers are being called upon to perform many new functions, including the consumption of homework formerly eaten by the dog.

Doug Larson, American columnist and editor

Computers, huh? I've heard it all boils down to just a bunch of ones and zeroes ... I don't know how that enables me to see naked women, but however it works, God bless you guys.

The King of Queens, CBS TV

If computers get too powerful, we can organise them into committees. That'll do them in.

Anon.

Never let a computer know you're in a hurry.

Anon.

Treat your password like your toothbrush. Don't let anybody else use it, and get a new one every six months.

Clifford Stoll, American astronomer and author

After growing wildly for years, the field of computing appears to be reaching its infancy.

John Pierce, American engineer and author

Hardware: where the people in your company's software section will tell you the problem is. Software: where the people in your company's hardware section will tell you the problem is.

Dave Barry, *Claw Your Way to the Top* (1986)

If you have any trouble sounding condescending, find a Unix user to show you how it's done.

Scott Adams, American cartoonist and creator of *Dilbert*

A computer lets you make more mistakes faster than any invention in human history – with the possible exceptions of handguns and tequila.

Mitch Ratcliffe, American journalist and entrepreneur

Don't anthropomorphise computers – they hate it.
  Anon.

A computer will do what you tell it to do, but that may be
much different from what you had in mind.
  Joseph Weizenbaum, German-American computer scientist

Jesus saves! The rest of us better make backups.
  Anon.

Truth is, I wouldn't know a gigabyte from a snakebite.
  Dolly Parton, American singer-songwriter

Computers are like air conditioners. They work fine until
you start opening windows.
  Anon.

Home is where you hang your @.
  Anon.

At least my pencil never crashes!
  Anon.

The Unix philosophy basically involves giving you just
enough rope to hang yourself. And then a couple of feet
more, just to be sure.
  Anon.

If Bill Gates had a penny for every time I've had to reboot
my computer ... oh my God, he does!
  Freddie Oliver, English comedian

One micro-computer maker was so successful, he had to move to smaller premises.

Max Kauffmann, American comedian

Closing all the internet windows by the time your boss gets to your desk is like getting the keys into the door before the killer gets you.

Facebook, 2012

When Bill Gates's life flashes before his eyes, I hope it appears as a PowerPoint presentation that employs every cheesy transition & effect.

Facebook, 2012

Once and for all, I agree to ALL the 'terms and conditions' that have or will ever exist!

Facebook, 2012

I work for the world's largest nanotechnology company. We're not very good.

Facebook, 2013

Pretty soon you'll be able to get married online, instead of saying 'I do' you will have to click 'I agree to these terms and conditions'.

Twitter, 2013

I'm going to become a hermit as soon as I find a cave with a decent Wi-Fi connection.

Anon.

I really love all the new features in Adobe Reader's eighth update today.

Facebook, 2012

Whom computers would destroy, they must first drive mad.

Anon.

A feature is a bug with seniority.

Anon.

Imagine if every Thursday your shoes exploded if you tied them the usual way. This happens to us all the time with computers, and nobody thinks of complaining.

Jef Raskin, American computer scientist and Macintosh guru

A computer is like an Old Testament god, with a lot of rules and no mercy.

Joseph Campbell, American author

Applying computer technology is simply finding the right wrench to pound in the correct screw.

Anon.

In a way, staring into a computer screen is like staring into an eclipse. It's brilliant and you don't realize the damage until it's too late.

Bruce Sterling, American science fiction author

Making duplicate copies and computer printouts of things no one wanted even one of in the first place is giving America a new sense of purpose.

Andy Rooney, television humorist

The best computer is a man, and it's the only one that can be mass-produced by unskilled labour.

Wernher von Braun, rocket scientist

The most overlooked advantage to owning a computer is that if they foul up, there's no law against whacking them around a little.

Joe Martin, *Porterfield* cartoon

The word user is the word used by the computer professional when they mean idiot.

Dave Barry, American author and columnist

There are many methods for predicting the future. For example, you can read horoscopes, tea leaves, tarot cards, or crystal balls. Collectively, these methods are known as 'nutty methods'. Or you can put well-researched facts into sophisticated computer models, more commonly referred to as a complete waste of time.

Scott Adams, American cartoonist and creator of *Dilbert*

It has been said that if you place an infinite amount of monkeys by one typewriter each, one of them will eventually write a literary masterpiece. The Internet has proven that this is not the case.

Anon.

Backup not found: (A)bort (R)etry (P)anic
  Anon.

All wiyht. Rho sritched mg kegtops awound?
  Anon.

I am far more annoyed at having to press the 'allow cook-ies' button on every website I visit than by anything cookies ever did to me.
  Twitter, 2012

When did 'fired up' become OK to say, instead of 'switched on'? It's a FUCKING LAPTOP. Not the pizza oven in Jamie Oliver's fucking garden.
  Ian Martin, British comedy writer

See also #COMPUTER PROGRAMMING, #INTERNET, #TWITTER, FACEBOOK AND SOCIAL MEDIA

#CONSULTANTS

Eight Ways to Spot a Consultant
1. A consultant is someone who's called in at the last minute to share the blame.
2. A consultant is someone who takes the watch off your wrist and tells you what time it is.
3. A consultant is simply an executive who can't find a job.
4. A consultant is a man who's smart enough to tell you how to run your own business and too smart to start one of his own.

5. A consultant is someone who saves his client almost enough to pay his fee.

6. A consultant is a man who knows 100 ways of making love but can't get a girl.

7. Those that can do. Those that could, but now don't, consult.

8. A consultant is a man sent in after the battle to bayonet the wounded.

Jerry Dennis, British comedian

Anyone who makes a business decision to hire a consultant, needs a consultant to help with their business decisions.

Anon.

If it ain't broke, don't fix it. Unless you're a consultant.

Anon.

Consult: to seek another's approval of a course already decided upon.

Ambrose Bierce, *The Devil's Dictionary* (1911)

See also #ADVICE

#CONTRACTS

A verbal agreement isn't worth the paper it's written on.

Louis B. Mayer, Hollywood producer

Contract: an agreement that is binding only on the weaker party.

Frederick Sawyer, American writer

#CREATIVITY

I make more mistakes than anyone else I know, and sooner or later, I patent most of them.

Thomas Edison, American inventor and scientist

Creativity is thinking up new things. Innovation is doing new things.

Theodore Levitt, American economist

The secret to creativity is knowing how to hide your sources.

Albert Einstein, German theoretical physicist

Creativity is allowing yourself to make mistakes. Art is knowing which ones to keep.

Scott Adams, American cartoonist and creator of *Dilbert*

Name the greatest of inventors?
Accident.

Mark Twain, American author

Don't think. Thinking is the enemy of creativity. It's self-conscious, and anything self-conscious is lousy. You can't try to do things. You simply must do things.

Ray Bradbury, American novelist

The thing we fear most in organizations – fluctuations, disturbances, imbalances – are the primary sources of creativity.

    Margaret J. Wheatley, American writer

Creativity is the sudden cessation of stupidity.

    Edwin Land, American scientist and inventor

Things are only impossible until they're not.

    Captain Jean-Luc Picard, *Star Trek: The Next Generation*

Anxiety is the hand maiden of creativity.

    T. S. Eliot, poet

Creativity always dies a quick death in rooms that house conference tables.

    Bruce Herschensohn, American political commentator

See also #IDEAS

#CREDIT

In God we trust. All others pay cash.

    Anon.

Preferential creditor: the first person to be told there's no money left.

    Anon.

There's only one problem with buying something on credit. By the time you're really sick of something, you finally own it.

Sally Poplin, British humorous writer

My credit is so bad, they won't even take my cash!

Jerry Dennis, British comedian

#CUSTOMERS

To all our nit-picky, over-demanding, ask-awkward-questions customers: Thank you and keep up the good work.

Advert for Dell Computers

There's a sucker born every minute.

Phineas T. Barnum, American circus owner

The consumer is not a moron, she is your wife.

David Ogilvy, ad man

The customer is frequently wrong. We write to them and say, 'Fly somebody else. Don't abuse our people!'

Herb Kelleher, co-founder of Southwest Airlines

Warning: Customers are Perishable.

Anon.

No one ever went broke underestimating the taste of the American public.

H. L. Mencken, American journalist

From this day forward, I solemnly promise and declare that every time a customer comes within ten feet of me, I will smile, look him in the eye and greet him, so help me Sam!

Sam Walton, founder of Walmart

A consumer is a shopper who is sore about something.

Harold Coffin, American scientist and academic

Never underestimate the power of the irate customer.

Anon.

See also #SALES AND SELLING

D

#DEBT

Never run into debt, not if you can find anything else to run into.

Josh Billings, American wit

I am having an out-of-money experience.

Anon.

Anyone who lives within his means suffers from a lack of imagination.

Oscar Wilde, Irish playwright

The only man who sticks closer to you in adversity than a friend is a creditor.

Anon.

Debt, *n*. An ingenious substitute for the chain and whip of the slave-driver.

Ambrose Bierce, *The Devil's Dictionary* (1911)

No man's credit is as good as his money.
  Edgar Watson Howe, American writer

Annual income twenty pounds, annual expenditure nineteen six, result happiness. Annual income twenty pounds, annual expenditure twenty pounds nought and six, result misery.
  Charles Dickens, *David Copperfield* (1849)

See also #BANKRUPTCY, #BORROWING AND LENDING

#DECISIONS

When I was a junior executive, the directors would always try to involve me in the decision-making process. Sometimes they even let me toss the coin.
  Freddie Oliver, English comedian

I have no plans and no plans to have plans.
  Mario Cuomo, Governor of New York 1983–94

A person always has two reasons for doing anything – a good reason, and the real reason.
  J. Pierpont Morgan, American banker and financier

If everyone is thinking alike then someone isn't thinking.
  George S. Patton, United States Army General

Indecision is the key to flexibility.
  Anon.

You may be sure that when a man begins to call himself a realist he is preparing to do something that he is secretly ashamed of doing.

Sydney J. Harris, American journalist

When you have to make a choice and don't make it, that is in itself a choice.

William James, American philosopher and psychologist

Consider what you think justice requires, and decide accordingly. But never give your reasons; for your judgment will probably be right, but your reasons will certainly be wrong.

Lord Mansfield, British barrister, politician and judge

A decision is what a man makes when he can't get anyone to serve on a committee.

Fletcher Knebel, American author

The hottest places in hell are reserved for those who, in times of great moral crisis, maintain their neutrality.

Dante, Italian poet

When a person tells you, 'I'll think it over and let you know' – you know.

Olin Miller, American humorist

All our final decisions are made in a state of mind that is not going to last.

Marcel Proust, French novelist

When I've heard all I need to make a decision, I don't take a vote. I make a decision.

Ronald Reagan, President of the United States 1981–89

When you come to a fork in the road, take it.

Yogi Berra, American baseball player and manager

There's nothing in the middle of the road but yellow stripes and dead armadillos.

Jim Hightower, Texas agricultural commissioner

E

#ECONOMICS

If you're not confused, you're not paying attention.
   Anon., *Wall Street Week*

There are three things not worth running for – a bus, a woman or a new economic panacea; if you wait a bit another one will come along.
   Derick Heathcoat-Amory, Chancellor of the Exchequer
   1958–60

Price, *n*. value, plus a reasonable sum for the wear and tear of conscience in demanding it.
   Ambrose Bierce, *The Devil's Dictionary* (1911)

One of the greatest pieces of economic wisdom is to know what you do not know.
   John Kenneth Galbraith, Canadian economist

An economist is a man who states the obvious in terms of the incomprehensible.

Alfred A. Knopf, American publisher

Inflation means that your money won't buy as much today as it did when you didn't have any.

Anon.

Waiting for supply-side economics to work is like leaving the landing lights on for Amelia Earhart.

Walter Heller, American economist

To have national prosperity we need to spend but to have individual prosperity we need to save.

Anon.

Economics is a subject that does not greatly respect one's wishes.

Nikita Khrushchev, Soviet Premier 1958–64

No real English gentleman, in his secret soul, was ever sorry for the death of a political economist.

Walter Bagehot, British economic and political journalist

Modern political theory seems to hold that the way to keep the economy in the pink is to run the country into the red.

Nathan Nielson, economist

The economy may suffer if auto sales drop – but that's the American way; we have to buy more cars than we need or we'll never be able to afford them.

  Jack Wilson, American businessman

Everything now seems to be under federal control except the national debt and the budget.

  Robert H. Goddard, American professor

A nation is not in danger of financial disaster merely because it owes itself money.

  Andrew W. Mellon, American banker

Economics is like being lost in the woods. How can you tell where you are going when you don't even know where you are?

  Anon.

Everybody is always in favour of general economy and particular expenditure.

  Anthony Eden, British Prime Minister 1955–57

The only function of economic forecasting is to make astrology look respectable.

  Anon.

Blessed are the young, for they shall inherit the national debt.

  Herbert Hoover, President of the United States 1929–33

I learned more about economics from one South Dakota dust storm than I did in all my years in college.

Hubert Humphrey, Vice-President of the United States 1965–69

If all economists were laid end to end, they would not reach a conclusion.

George Bernard Shaw, Irish playwright

Economics is extremely useful as a form of employment for economists.

John Kenneth Galbraith, Canadian economist

We can safely abandon the basic doctrine of the '80s: namely that the rich were not working because they had too little money, the poor because they had too much.

John Kenneth Galbraith, Canadian economist

Economics is an entire scientific discipline of not knowing what you're talking about.

P. J. O'Rourke, *Eat the Rich* (1998)

An economist is someone who sees something that works in practice and wonders if it would work in theory.

Ronald Reagan, President of the United States 1981–89

A friend of mine was asked to a costume ball a short time ago. He slapped some egg on his face and went as a liberal economist.

Ronald Reagan, President of the United States 1981–89

Saying we're in a slow recovery, not a recession, is like saying we don't have any unemployed – we just have a lot of people who are really, really late for work.

Jay Leno, American television host

A recession is what takes the wind out of your sales.

Anon.

Don't forget, economists have accurately forecast nine out of the last five recessions.

Anon.

Is there going to be a devaluation?
That's the $63,000 question.

Anon.

Prosperity is something that businessmen create for politicians to take the credit for.

Anon.

There are three types of economist in the world: those who can count and those who can't.

Eddie George, Governor of the Bank of England
1993–2003

Trickle down. The whole theory was this: We have all the money. If we drop some, it's yours. Go for it.

Bill Maher, American television host

It is not possible for this nation to be at once politically internationalist and economically isolationist. This is just as insane as asking one Siamese twin to high dive while the other plays the piano.

Adlai Stevenson, American politician

Nobody who has wealth to distribute ever omits himself.

Leon Trotsky, Russian Marxist revolutionary

It's a recession when your neighbor loses his job; it's a depression when you lose your own.

Harry S. Truman, President of the United States 1945–53

The way to stop financial joy-riding is to arrest the chauffeur, not the automobile.

Woodrow Wilson, President of the United States 1913–21

I believe that economists put decimal points in their forecasts to show they have a sense of humor.

William E. Simon, American businessman and Secretary of the Treasury

If economists were any good at business, they would be rich men instead of advisors to rich men.

Kirk Kerkorian, Hollywood mogul

In all recorded history there has not been one economist who had to worry where the next meal would come from.

Peter Drucker, American businessman and author

An economist's guess is as likely to be as good as anybody else's.

Will Rogers, American humorist

#ENTREPRENEURS

'The Enterprise Model'
Some regard private enterprise as if it were a predatory tiger to be shot.
Others look upon it as a cow that they can milk.
Only a handful see it for what it really is – the strong horse that pulls the whole cart.

Winston Churchill, British statesman and orator

'The European Social Model'
The main aim for a businessman in Europe, it seems to me, is to try and make money faster than the government can take it away from you.
There have, of course, been entrepreneurs since almost the beginning of time. Noah, for instance, managed to float a company when the whole world was in liquidation.

Winston Churchill, British statesman and orator

I've not failed. I've just found ten thousand ways that won't work.

Thomas Edison, American inventor and scientist

It is not because things are difficult that we do not dare; it is because we do not dare that they are difficult.

Seneca, Roman philosopher and statesman

Entrepreneurs can be divided into two types: those who don't take tranquilisers – the nervous wrecks – and those who do – the calm wrecks.

Anon.

Everything is always impossible before it works.
That is what entrepreneurs are all about – doing what people have told them is impossible.

R. Hunt Greene, American venture capitalist

A man isn't a man until he has to meet a payroll.

Ivan Shaffer, American writer

Good entrepreneurs, like good tea, can only be appreciated when they're in hot water.

Anon.

Take the obvious, add a cupful of brains, a generous pinch of imagination, a bucketful of courage and daring, stir well and bring to a boil.

Bernard Baruch, American financier and statesman, on enterprise

The reason a lot of people do not recognise opportunity is because it usually goes around wearing overalls looking like hard work.

Thomas Edison, American inventor and scientist

I reckon one entrepreneur can recognise another at 300 yards on a misty day.

Peter Parker, British businessman

When trouble arises and things look bad, there is always one individual who perceives a solution and is willing to take command.
Very often that individual is crazy.

Dave Barry, American author and columnist

No one can achieve any real or lasting success or 'get rich' in business by being a conformist.

J. Paul Getty, American industrialist

I'm a self-made man but I think if I had to do it all again, I'd give the job to someone else.

Roland Young, English actor

Where would the Rockefellers be today if old John D. had gone on selling short-weight kerosene to widows and orphans instead of wisely deciding to mulct the whole country?

S. J. Perelman, American humorist

If you want to understand entrepreneurs, you have to study the psychology of the juvenile delinquent.
They don't have the same anxiety triggers that we have.

Abraham Zalesnik, American psychologist

The ideal of the employer is to have products without employees.
The ideal of the employee is to have income without work.

E. F. Schumacher, economic thinker and statistician

The entrepreneur is like an eagle: he soars alone, he flies alone, he hunts alone.

Dr Michael Smurfit, Irish businessman

Winning isn't everything, But *wanting* to win is.

Arnold Palmer, golfer

It sounds boring but anything is easy to start – starting a novel, starting a business ... it's keeping the thing going that is difficult.

Prue Leith, English chef and entrepreneur

If you want to be a successful entrepreneur, you've got to be a bad loser.
You know what they say, 'Show me a good loser and I'll show you a loser.'

Anon.

Every successful enterprise requires three men: a dreamer, a businessman and a son of a bitch.

Peter McArthur, newspaper publisher

Follow the crowd and you'll never be followed by a crowd.

Anon.

If the creator had a purpose in equipping us with a neck, he surely meant for us to stick it out.

Arthur Koestler, author and journalist

#ETHICS

Live in such a way that you would not be afraid to sell your parrot to the town gossip.
   Will Rogers, American humorist

An ethical man is a Christian holding four aces.
   Mark Twain, American author

Any preoccupation with ideas of what is right or wrong in conduct shows an arrested intellectual development.
   Oscar Wilde, *Phrases and Philosophies for the Use of the Young* (1894)

First secure an independent income, then practise virtue.
   Greek proverb

What is moral is what you feel good after.
   Ernest Hemingway, American author

Living with a conscience is like driving a car with the brakes on.
   Budd Schulberg, American humorist

The best way to keep one's word is not to give it.
   Napoleon Bonaparte, French military and political leader

Man is the only animal that blushes – or needs to.
   Mark Twain, American author

Never believe anything until it has been officially denied.
    Claud Cockburn, British journalist

Conscience is the inner voice that warns us that someone
may be looking.
    H. L. Mencken, American journalist

Ethics stays in the preface of the average business science
book.
    Peter Drucker, American businessman and author

We should keep the Panama Canal. After all, we stole it fair
and square.
    S. I. Hayakawa, American senator

#EUROPE AND THE EU

Some day, following the example of the United States of
America, there will be a United States of Europe.
    George Washington, first President of the United States
    1789–97

But the age of chivalry is gone. That of sophisters, economists, and calculators has succeeded; and the glory of
Europe is extinguished forever.
    Edmund Burke, Irish statesman and philosopher

Europe's the mayonnaise, but America supplies the good
old lobster.
    D. H. Lawrence, English writer

To understand Europe, you have to be a genius – or French.
  Madeleine Albright, first female US Secretary of State
  1997–2001

The euro is a sickly premature infant, the result of an over-hasty monetary union.
  Gerhard Schröder, German opposition leader, March 1998

I have always found the word 'Europe' on the lips of those who wanted something from others which they dared not demand in their own names!
  Otto von Bismarck, Chancellor of Germany 1871–90

To enter Europe, you must have a valid passport with a photograph of yourself in which you look like you are being booked on charges of soliciting sheep.
  Dave Barry, American author and columnist

Who do I call if I want to call Europe?
  Henry Kissinger, American diplomat

They spell it *Vinci* and pronounce it *Vinchy*, foreigners always spell better than they pronounce.
  Mark Twain, American author

Boy, those French! They have a different word for everything!
  Steve Martin, American comedian

There is no freedom in Europe – that's certain – it is besides a worn-out portion of the globe.
  Lord Byron, English Romantic poet

No accident that debacle is a French word.

John Lanchester, *The Debt to Pleasure* (1996)

The last time Britain went into Europe with any degree of success was on 6 June 1944.

Daily Express (1980)

What Caesar couldn't do, what Charlemagne couldn't do, what Innocent III and Hitler couldn't do, it looks like the dough-faced burgher wimps of Brussels might finally be able to pull off – the unification of that portion of the earth's surface known ... as Europe. What it took a country ten times its size less than a hundred years to accomplish, armed with only machine guns and a few trillion dollars, it has taken the squabbling, babbling tribes of Europe almost three millennia of wars, migrations, crusades, plague, pillage, partition, diets, dumas, duels, vendettas, incursions, invasions, intrusions, regicides, switching sides and genocide to accomplish.

Tony Hendra, 'EEC! It's the US of E!', *National Lampoon* (1976)

I do not find northern Europe an ideal zone for human habitation. It is a fine place for industrial productivity, but its climate breeds puritans and the terrible dictates of the Protestant Work Ethic. The Romans were right to pull out when they did.

Kenneth Tynan, *The Sound of Two Hands Clapping* (1975)

I don't hold with abroad and think that foreigners speak English when our backs are turned.

Quentin Crisp, *The Naked Civil Servant* (1968)

I do not see the EEC as a great love affair. It is more like nine middle-aged couples with failing marriages meeting at a Brussels hotel for a group grope.

Kenneth Tynan, English writer and critic

European Community institutions have produced European beets, butter, cheese, wine, veal and even pigs. But they have not produced Europeans.

Louise Weiss, French author and MEP

Gloria, gloria, Europhoria!
Common faith and common goal!
Meat and milk and wine and butter
Make a smashing casserole!
Let the end of all our striving
Be the peace that love promotes,
With our hands in perfect friendship
Firmly round each other's throats!

Roger Woddis, *Spectator* (1984)

#EXPENSES

In Brighton she was Brenda,
She was Patsy up in Perth,
In Cambridge she was Candida
The sweetest girl on earth.
In Stafford she was Stella,
The pick of all the bunch,
But down on his expenses,
She was *Petrol, Oil and Lunch*.

Anon.

See also #ACCOUNTANCY, #BUDGETS, #TAXATION

#EXPERIENCE

Experience is the comb life gives you after you've lost your hair.
Anon.

We learn from experience that men never learn anything from experience.
George Bernard Shaw, Irish playwright

An old poacher makes a good gamekeeper.
Anon.

The hardest thing to learn in life is which bridge to cross and which to burn.
David L. Russell, American educator

What a man knows at fifty which he didn't know at twenty is, for the most part, incommunicable.
Adlai Stevenson, American politician

Experience is something you don't get until just after you need it.
Steven Wright, American comedian

You must learn from the mistakes of others. You can't possibly live long enough to make them all yourself.
Sam Levenson, American humorist

I don't want men of experience working for me. The experienced man is always telling me why something can't be done. He is smart, he is intelligent, he thinks he knows the answers. The fellow who has not had any experience is so dumb he doesn't know a thing can't be done – and he goes ahead and does it.

Charles F. Kettering, American engineer and inventor

Experience is the worst teacher; it gives the test before presenting the lesson.

Vernon S. Law, baseball player and preacher

A man who carries a cat by the tail learns something he can learn in no other way.

Mark Twain, American author

Human beings, who are almost unique in having the ability to learn from the experience of others, are also remarkable for their apparent disinclination to do so.

Douglas Adams, British comedy writer

The best substitute for experience is being sixteen.

Anon.

Never insult an alligator until you've crossed the river.

Cordell Hull, United States Secretary of State

To most men, experience is like the stern lights of a ship which illumine only the track it has passed.

Samuel Taylor Coleridge, English writer

F

#FAILURE

Failure is the greatest opportunity I have to know who I really am.

John Killinger, Republican politician from Pennsylvania

Failure is only the opportunity to begin again, more intelligently.

Henry Ford, American industrialist

No one knows what to say in the loser's room.

Muhammad Ali, boxer

I don't know if getting everything I want would make me happy, but the opposite is not working at all!

Pinterest, 2013

I started out with nothing – and I've still got most of it left.

Anon.

It is a lonesome walk to the sidelines, especially when thousands of people are cheering your replacement.

Fran Tarkenton, quarterback, Minnesota Vikings

There is much to be said for failure. It is more interesting than success.

Max Beerbohm, *Mainly on the Air* (1947)

It is hard to fail, but it is worse never to have tried to succeed.

Theodore Roosevelt, President of the United States
1901–09

Started from the bottom. Still pretty much there...

Twitter, 2013

I didn't fail the test, I just found 100 ways to do it wrong.

Benjamin Franklin, polymath and Founding Father of the
United States

Never confuse a single defeat with a final defeat.

F. Scott Fitzgerald, American novelist

I never fail. It's just that the people around me succeed more than I.

Carroll Bryant, author and songwriter

At some time in the lifecycle of every organization, its ability to succeed in spite of itself runs out.

Frederick Sawyer, American writer

If at first you don't succeed; you are running about average.
M. H. Alderson, publisher, *Reader's Digest*

He has hit rock bottom and started to dig.
Anon.

[Of a fellow playwright:] That poor man. He's completely unspoiled by failure.
Noël Coward, English playwright

There is the greatest practical benefit in making a few failures early in life.
T. H. Huxley, *On Medical Education* (1870)

Failure has gone to his head.
Wilson Mizner, of a still-buoyant bankrupt.

If I were not a gloriously successful person, in England they would have dismissed me as an Irishman and in America as a Socialist.
George Bernard Shaw, Irish playwright.

See also #MISTAKES, #SUCCESS, #SUCCESS AND FAILURE

#FINANCE

A holding company is the people you give your money to while you're being searched.
Will Rogers, American humorist

Profits are part of the mechanism by which society decides what it wants to see produced.

   Henry C. Wallich, American economist

If profits are evil, losses must be ten times worse.

   Anon.

He's got a wonderful head for money. There's a long slit on the top.

   Anon.

Budget: a mathematical confirmation of your suspicions.

   A. A. Latimer, American politician

See also #ACCOUNTANCY, #BANKS AND BANKING

G

#GOALS

Goals are dreams with deadlines.
  Anon.

Chandler: Hey, you guys in the living room all know what you want to do. You know, you have goals. You have dreams. I don't have a dream.
Ross: Ah, the lesser known 'I Don't Have a Dream' speech.
  'The One with the Stoned Guy', *Friends* (1996)

Some of the world's greatest feats were accomplished by people not smart enough to know they were impossible.
  Doug Larson, American columnist and editor

I love deadlines. I like the whooshing sound they make as they fly by.
  Douglas Adams, British comedy writer

To be sure of hitting the target, shoot first and call whatever you hit the target.
  Anon.

The question isn't who is going to let me; it's who is going to stop me.

    Ayn Rand, *The Fountainhead* (1943)

The greatest dreams are always unrealistic.

    Will Smith, American actor and producer

The only thing that has to be finished by next Tuesday is next Monday.

    Jennifer Yane, American artist

Establishing goals is all right if you don't let them deprive you of interesting detours.

    Doug Larson, American columnist and editor

We're still not where we're going, but we're not where we were.

    Natasha Josefowitz, American author and poet

There are no shortcuts to any place worth going.

    Beverly Sills, American operatic soprano

Nothing interferes with my concentration. You could put on an orgy in my office and I wouldn't look up. Well, maybe once.

    Isaac Asimov, academic and science fiction author

See also #AMBITION

#GOLF

I can tell more about how someone is likely to react in a business situation from one round of golf than I can from a hundred hours of meetings.

Mark McCormack, *What They Don't Teach You at Harvard Business School* (1988)

You can know a guy for twenty years and not realise he's a jerk until you've played a round of golf with him. Would you really want to invest your life savings with someone who had just toed his ball into a better line when he thought you weren't looking?
No. But you might want to retain him as your lawyer.

David Owen, *My Usual Game* (1995)

It's amazing how many people beat you at golf now you're no longer president.

George H. W. Bush, President of the United States 1989–93

If people are golfers and their handicap doesn't go up, they're not doing their job.

Eli Broad, American businessman

Golf is played by twenty million mature American men whose wives think they are out having fun.

Jim Bishop, American journalist and author

Don't play too much golf. Two rounds a day are plenty.

Harry Vardon, professional golfer

A: Why aren't you playing golf with your boss anymore?

B: What! Would *you* play with a man who swears and curses with every shot, who cheats in the bunkers and who enters false scores on his cards?

A: Certainly not!

B: Well neither will my boss.

Freddie Oliver, English comedian

Golf is a game whose aim is to hit a very small ball into an even smaller hole with weapons singularly ill-designed for the purpose.

Winston Churchill, British statesman and orator

See also #RETIREMENT

#GOVERNMENT

The business of government is to keep the government out of business – that is, unless business needs government aid.

Will Rogers, American humorist

The government is best that governs least.

Thomas Jefferson, Founding Father and President of the United States 1801–09

Be thankful we're not getting all the government we're paying for.

Will Rogers, American humorist

I learned in business that you had to be very careful when you told somebody that's working for you to do something, because the chances were very high he'd do it. In government, you don't have to worry about that.

George Shultz, American economist, statesman and
businessman

The single most exciting thing you encounter in government is competence, because it's so rare.

Daniel Patrick Moynihan, American Democratic politician
and sociologist

The government solution to a problem is usually as bad as the problem.

Milton Friedman, American economist

Put a federal agency in charge of the Sahara Desert and it would run out of sand.

Peggy Noonan, presidential speechwriter

Giving money and power to the government is like giving whisky and car keys to teenage boys.

P. J. O'Rourke, *Parliament of Whores* (1991)

You know, if government were a product, selling it would be illegal.

P. J. O'Rourke, American political satirist and author

The nine most terrifying words in the English language are 'I'm from the government and I'm here to help.'

Ronald Reagan, President of the United States 1981–89

H

#HIRING AND FIRING

Nothing bad's going to happen to us. If we get fired, it's not failure. It's a midlife vocational reassessment.

P. J. O'Rourke, American political satirist and author

Job interview tip: Tell them you're not an applicant, you're an appliCAN. Lick your finger, hold it against buttock. Make sizzling noise.

Twitter, 2013

'You're fired!' No other words can so easily and succinctly reduce a confident, self-assured executive to an insecure, grovelling shred of his former self.

Frank P. Louchheim, 'The Art of Getting Fired' (1984)

There's nothing so improves the mood of the party as the imminent execution of a senior colleague.

Alan Clark, British politician

I am looking for a lot of men who have an infinite capacity to not know what can't be done.

Henry Ford, American industrialist

The Sack and How to Give It
- I just don't know what we'd do without you. But we're going to try.
- Tell me, how long have you been with us – not counting tomorrow.
- You'll find a little extra in your pay packet this week – your cards.
- Look, you made a mistake and I'd like to help you out. Which way did you come in?
- The official reason you're leaving is because of illness and fatigue. I'm sick and tired of you.
- Look, you made a mistake but it's not a resigning matter. Not at all. You're fired!
- We're extending our flexi-time experiment. From today you can go home any time you like – and stay there.
- You've got that resigned look about you again.
- This time, why don't you put it in writing?
- Despite all the suggestions I've made over the years, I've never been able to fire you with enthusiasm. Until now.

David Frost, 'The Sack and How to Give It', *We British* (1975)

'I quit because the boss used repulsive language.'
'What did he say?'
'He said, "You're fired!"'

Anon.

She works well when under constant supervision and cornered like a rat in a trap.
   Excerpt from testimonial, Lussac les Chateaux, France

The closest to perfection a man comes is when he fills in a job application.
   Anon.

A résumé is a balance sheet without any liabilities.
   Robert Half, American business executive

Everybody looks good on paper.
   John Y. Brown, American business executive and governor of Kentucky

See also #HUMAN RESOURCES, #UNEMPLOYMENT

#HUMAN RESOURCES

Excerpts from Employee Evaluations:
- I would not breed from this employee.
- He would be out of his depth in a car-park puddle.
- This man is depriving a village somewhere of an idiot.
- He has the wisdom of youth and the energy of old age.
- This young lady has delusions of adequacy.
- She sets low personal standards and then consistently fails to achieve them.
- If she were any stupider, she'd have to be watered twice a week.

- He's a prime candidate for natural deselection.
- This man must have entered the gene pool while the life-guard wasn't watching.

  Anon.

Never hire anybody whose CV rhymes.

  Rita Rudner, American comedian

Employer-Speak
- Join our fast-paced team = We have no time to train you
- Duties will vary = Anyone in the office can boss you around
- Must have an eye for detail = We have no quality control
- Must be deadline-orientated = You'll be six months behind schedule on your first day
- Apply in person = If you're old or fat or ugly, you'll be told the position has been filled
- Competitive salary = We remain competitive by paying less than our competitors
- Requires team leadership skills = You'll have the respon-sibilities of a manager without the pay or respect
- Problem-solving skills a must = This is a company in perpetual chaos

  Anon.

Employee-Speak
- I am adaptable = I've changed jobs a lot
- I take pride in my work = I blame others for my mistakes
- I'm extremely experienced in all aspects of office organi-sation = I've used Microsoft Office

- I am always on the go = I'm never at my desk
- I'm highly motivated to succeed = The minute I find a better job, I'm gone

  Anon.

Personnel manager: I like your qualifications, Gribson – you have the makings of a first-class underling.

  Hector Breeze, British cartoonist

I took one of those job-assessment tests at work the other day. The report said my aptitudes and abilities were best suited to some form of early retirement.

  Anon.

I've used up all my sick days so I'm calling in dead.

  Anon.

Restructuring: A simple plan instituted from above in which workers are right-sized, downsized, surplused, lateralised or, in the business jargon of the days of yore, fired.

  Anon.

We have a guy in our office who accumulates a lot of absenteeism. I said to the boss one day, 'Why don't you fire him?' He said, 'Fire him? I don't even know what he looks like! I'll give you an idea how often he turns up at work. His nickname in the office is "Halley's Comet".'
The guy was absent so much, we held his retirement party at his house.

  Gene Perret, American joke writer

Few great men would have got past Personnel.
   Paul Goodman, American journalist

See also #HIRING AND FIRING, #UNEMPLOYMENT

I

#IDEAS

Ideas are useless unless used.
    Theodore Levitt, American economist

I can't understand why people are frightened of new ideas.
I'm frightened of the old ones.
    John Cage, American composer

Nothing is more dangerous than an idea when you only
have one idea.
    Emile-August Chartier, French philosopher

Man's mind, stretched to a new idea, never goes back to its
original dimensions.
    Oliver Wendell Holmes, American physician and poet

Exhilaration is that feeling you get just after a great idea
hits you and before you realise what's wrong with it.
    Rex Harrison, English actor

Every man with an idea has at least two or three followers.

Brooks Atkinson, *Once Around the Sun* (1951)

If you have an apple and I have an apple and we exchange these apples then you and I will still each have one apple. But if you have an idea and I have an idea and we exchange these ideas, then each of us will have two ideas.

George Bernard Shaw, Irish playwright

A new idea is delicate. It can be killed by a sneer or a yawn; it can be stabbed to death by a quip and worried to death by a frown on the right man's brow.

Charles Brower, advertising man

If at first, the idea is not absurd, then there is no hope for it.

Albert Einstein, German theoretical physicist

A pile of rocks ceases to be a rock when somebody contemplates it with the idea of a cathedral in mind.

Antoine de Saint-Exupéry, French aristocrat and poet

Night time is really the best time to work. All the ideas are there to be yours because everyone else is asleep.

Catherine O'Hara, actress, writer and comedian

The ideas I stand for are not mine. I borrowed them from Socrates. I swiped them from Chesterfield. I stole them from Jesus. And I put them in a book. If you don't like their rules, whose would you use?

Dale Carnegie, self-help author

Adults are always asking little kids what they want to be when they grow up because they're looking for ideas.

Paula Poundstone, American comedian

No one ever had an idea in a dress suit.

Frederick G. Banting, Canadian medical scientist and discoverer of insulin

An idea isn't responsible for the people who believe in it.

Don Marquis, American journalist

Every really new idea looks crazy at first.

Alfred North Whitehead, *An Introduction to Mathematics* (1911)

Never dump a good idea on a conference table. It will belong to the conference.

Jane Trahey, American copywriter and author

Never invest in an idea you can't illustrate with a crayon.

Peter Lynch, American businessman

Ideas are like rabbits. You get a couple and learn how to handle them and pretty soon you have a dozen.

John Steinbeck, American novelist

You are always going to have people who copy things that work.

Jay S. Walker, American entrepreneur

All the really good ideas I ever had came to me while milking a cow.

    Grant Wood, American painter

An idea that is not dangerous is unworthy of being called an idea at all.

    Oscar Wilde, Irish playwright

The best way to kill an idea is to take it to a meeting.

    Anon.

See also #CREATIVITY

#INCOME

It is better to have a permanent income than to be fascinating.

    Oscar Wilde, Irish playwright

There is only one thing for a man to do who is married to a woman who enjoys spending money and that is to enjoy earning it.

    Edgar Watson Howe, American writer

At the Bitter End, my salary was in the high two figures.

    Woody Allen, actor and writer, on a New York nightclub at which he performed

#INFLATION

Among the things that money can't buy is what it used to.
  Max Kauffmann, American comedian

Time for belt-tightening. You can't live on a million a year anymore.
  Randy Newman, American songwriter

Americans are getting stronger. Twenty years ago, it took two people to carry ten dollars' worth of groceries. Today, a five-year-old can do it.
  Henny Youngman, American comedian

You know you've got inflation when one can live as cheaply as two.
  Anon.

The economy hasn't reached rock-bottom yet – but if we keep climbing, it soon will.
  Anon.

A deficit is what you have when you haven't as much as you had when you had nothing.
  Anon.

A friend of mine told me, 'I'm determined to stay out of debt – even if I have to borrow money to do so.'
  Anon.

A guy said to me today, 'I assume you're against inflation.'
I said, 'Absolutely – 300 per cent!'

Anon.

#INSULTS

What he lacks in intelligence, he makes up for in stupidity.

Anon.

A day away from Tallulah [Bankhead] is like a month in
the country.

Howard Dietz, American lyricist

I won't eat anything that has intelligent life but I would
gladly eat a network executive or a politician.

Marty Feldman, English writer and comedian

He's a few peas short of a pod.
He's a sandwich short of a picnic.
She's a couplet short of a sonnet.
He couldn't pour water out of a boot even if the instruc-
    tions were written on the heel.
His mouth is in gear but his brain is in neutral.
She's knitting with only one needle.
If his IQ were two points higher, he'd be a rock.
Somebody's blown out his pilot light.
He's suffering from Clue Deficit Disorder.

Anon.

I'd say the wheel's spinning but the hamster's dead.
His aerial doesn't pick up all the channels.
All booster, no payload.
He's a few fries short of a Happy Meal.
He doesn't have all his dogs on the same leash.
He's all foam and no beer.
I'm afraid her receiver's off the hook.
He's got an IQ that's about room temperature.
He doesn't have the brainpower to toast a crouton.
A flash of light, a cloud of dust and what was the question?

Anon.

If idiots could fly, this place would be an airport.

Anon.

Every year he finishes last in the company popularity poll.
And he only finishes that high because he votes for himself.

Anon.

He's a man who has no equals – only superiors.

Anon.

He's a self-made man who obviously gave the job to the lowest bidder.

Anon.

He's someone who can bring an atmosphere of happiness, laughter and merriment into the office – simply by being absent.

Sally Poplin, British humorous writer

His boss stopped him having his five-minute tea-breaks. It was taking too long to retrain him.

Anon.

His main problem? He has delusions of adequacy.

Anon.

Why are there so many more horses' asses than there are horses?

G. Gordon Liddy, American lawyer and Watergate conspiracist

A bore is someone who follows your joke with a better one.

Anon.

Nobody ever forgets where he buried a hatchet.

Kin Hubbard, American humorist

No one has a higher opinion of him than I have – and I think he's third-rate.

Jerry Dennis, British comedian

#INSURANCE

I've got a very special fire and theft insurance.
It only pays out if I'm robbed while my house is burning.

Anon.

Accidents will happen. Unless you have an accident policy.

Sally Poplin, British humorous writer

An insurance salesman just signed me up for a marvellous retirement policy. If I keep up the payments for ten years, he can retire.

Anon.

BUPA? That's the company that docks my pay to pay my doc.

Anon.

I'm with an extremely reliable insurance company. In all the thirty years I've been with them, they've never missed sending me the bill.

Anon.

I've got an extremely comprehensive health-insurance policy. For instance, if I should ever come down with yellow fever, they'll repaint my bedroom so I don't clash with the walls.

Sally Poplin, British humorous writer

I've got no-fault car insurance. If I have an accident, I just call the insurance company and they tell me it isn't their fault.

Max Kauffmann, American comedian

Perhaps someone can help me.
I've got this new life-insurance policy, but I don't understand the small print. The only thing I know is that after I die, I can stop paying.

Anon.

I've got wonderful health insurance. If I ever get knocked on the head, they pay me a lump sum.

Anon.

In every insurance policy, the big print giveth and the small print taketh away.

Anon.

Insurance is what keeps you poor so you can die rich.

Anon.

People who live in glass houses should take out insurance.

Anon.

A friend of mine had two wooden legs. One day his house burned down and unfortunately his legs got caught in the blaze. But the insurance company refused to pay up. They said he didn't have a leg to stand on.

Anon.

Insurance: an ingenious modem game of chance in which the player is permitted to enjoy the comfortable conviction that he is beating the man who keeps the table.

Ambrose Bierce, *The Devil's Dictionary* (1911)

I took a physical for some life insurance.
All they would give me was fire and theft.

Sally Poplin, British humorous writer

But my agent said the policy *would* cover me falling off the roof.

But it doesn't cover me hitting the ground.

Max Kauffmann, American comedian

I detest life insurance agents. They always argue that I shall some day die, which is not so.

Stephen Leacock, *Literary Lapses* (1910)

I don't want to tell you how much insurance I carry with the Prudential, but all I can say is: when I go, *they* go.

Jack Benny, American comedian

... the Act of God designation on all insurance policies; which means roughly, that you cannot be insured for the accidents that are most likely to happen to you. If your ox kicks a hole in your neighbour's Maserati, however, indemnity is instantaneous.

Alan Coren, *The Lady from Stalingrad Mansions* (1977)

#INTERNET

Dear Google: Please stop being like my wife. Kindly let me complete my sentence before you start to give me suggestions.

Facebook, 2010

It's Google's 15th birthday today. Typical fifteen-year-old. It's got an answer for everything.

Twitter, 2013

According to a survey, 85 per cent of men admit they surf the internet wearing nothing but their underwear. 63 per cent said that's how they lost their last job.

Jay Leno, American television host

On the internet, nobody knows you're a dog.

Peter Steiner, *New Yorker* cartoon

If Internet Explorer is brave enough to ask to be your default browser, you're brave enough to ask that girl out.

Facebook, 2013

Getting information off the internet is like taking a drink from a fire hydrant.

Mitchell Kapor, personal computing pioneer

See also #COMPUTERS, #TWITTER, FACEBOOK AND SOCIAL MEDIA

#INVESTMENT AND THE STOCK MARKET

If you don't make a profit from your investment mistakes, someone else will.

Yale Hirsch, Wall Street publisher

The only safe way to double your money is to fold it over once and put it in your pocket.

Anon.

$1,000, left to earn interest at 8 per cent a year, will grow to 43 quadrillion in 400 years. But the first hundred years are the toughest.

Sidney Homer, Salomon Brothers analyst

Gentlemen prefer bonds.

Andrew Mellon, American banker and philanthropist

There are two times in a man's life when he should not speculate – when he can't afford it and when he can.

Mark Twain, American author

I used to think my broker was bearish. Then I thought he was bullish. Now I just think that he's rubbish.

Anon.

My stockbrokers are a legend in the City for accurately predicting the 1929 crash – sixty years too late.

Anon.

The stock market was in a terrible state last year. One day the Dow Jones was unchanged and they called it a rally.

Max Kauffmann, American comedian

Choose stocks the way porcupines make love – very carefully.

Anon.

Now is always the most difficult time to invest.

Anon.

Now I'm really in trouble. The laundry just rang me to tell me they've lost my shirt. And my broker called to say the same thing.

Max Kauffmann, American comedian

Rules for playing the stock market:
Rule 1: Don't panic
Rule 2: Panic first.

Walter Russell Mead, economist, *Esquire*, October 1998

It is not the return *on* my investment that I am concerned about; it is the return *of* my investment.

Will Rogers, American humorist

Can we trust the City anymore? The way things are going, the future of 'invest' seems to be 'investigation'.

Anon.

There was a tremendous turnaround in the market today. A stockbroker who jumped out of a window on the twelfth floor saw a computer screen on the seventh floor and did a U-turn.

Anon.

They call him a broker because, after you see him, you are.

Anon.

Wall Street had just voted him Man of the Year. Unfortunately the year is 1929.

Anon.

When I saw how badly my shares were doing, I tried to call my broker – but his ledge was busy.

    Anon.

You know you've gone to the wrong stockbroker when you ask him to buy you 1,000 shares in IBM and he asks you how to spell it.

    Jerry Dennis, British comedian

One of the funny things about the stock market is that every time one person buys, another sells, and they both think they are being astute.

    Sally Poplin, British humorous writer

October: This is one of the peculiarly dangerous months to speculate in stocks in. The others are July, January, September, April, November, May, March, June, December, August and February.

    Mark Twain, *Pudd'nhead Wilson* (1894)

See also #FINANCE

L

#LAW, THE

No brilliance is needed in the law. Nothing but common sense, and relatively clean fingernails.

John Mortimer, *A Voyage Round My Father* (1972)

For certain people, after fifty, litigation takes the place of sex.

Gore Vidal, American writer and political commentator

I know of no method to secure the repeal of bad or obnoxious laws so effective as their stringent execution.

Ulysses S. Grant, President of the United States 1869–77

Defendant: I don't recognise this court!
Judge: Why not?
Defendant: You've had it decorated!

Eric Morecambe and Ernie Wise, *The Morecambe and Wise Joke Book* (1979)

I don't want a lawyer to tell me what I cannot do; I hire him to tell me how to do what I want to do.

J. Pierpont Morgan, American banker and financier

Morgenhall: ... if they ever give you a brief, old fellow, attack the medical evidence. Remember, the jury's full of rheumatism and arthritis and shocking gastric troubles. They love to see a medical man put through it.

John Mortimer, *The Dock Brief* (1958)

Judge: Don't take that 'judge not, lest ye be judged' line with *me*, young man.

Gahan Wilson, *The Weird World of Gahan Wilson* (1975)

That's what comes of being a solicitor, it saps the vital juices. Johnny doesn't even embezzle his clients' money, which I should have thought was about the only fun a solicitor can get out of life.

P. G. Wodehouse, *Ice in the Bedroom* (1961)

Pride comes before a fall – compensation comes after.

Anon.

Lawyer: To save the state the expense of a trial, Your Honor, my client has escaped.

Chon Day, *New Yorker*, cartoon

Juries scare me. I don't want to put my faith in twelve people who weren't smart enough to get out of jury duty.

Monica Piper, American writer, actress and comedian

A judge is a man who ends a sentence with a sentence.

Anon.

A jury is one thing that never works properly after it's been fixed.

Anon.

A jury is twelve people whose job it is to decide which side has the better lawyer.

Robert Frost, American poet

A jury is a group of citizens who will try anyone once.

Jerry Dennis, British comedian

He became a High Court judge – an honour few people receive while they're still alive.

Anon.

I began to get suspicious of the contract when I saw that the first paragraph forbade you from reading any of the others.

Anon.

I don't understand. How come they lock the jury up overnight and let the prisoner go home?

Anon.

I thought I was intelligent until I was tried by a jury of my peers.

Frederick Sawyer

If you can't get a lawyer who knows the law, get one who knows the judge.

Anon.

In the old days there was one law for the rich and one law for the poor. Today there are thousands of laws for everyone.

Anon.

It takes a thief to catch a thief – and a jury to let him go.

Anon.

These days we'll try anything once – except criminals.

Jerry Dennis, British comedian

Judge: There's far too much of this sexual intercourse going on. And I'm not having it!

Anon.

The Old Bailey, where justice is dispensed with.

Anon.

What causes all this trouble is that we have 10,000 laws to enforce the Ten Commandments.

Jerry Dennis, British comedian

What's the difference between unlawful and illegal? Unlawful is against the law. Illegal is a sick bird.

Anon.

You've been found guilty of not stopping at a red light. Do you have anything to say in mitigation?

Well, I've often stopped at green lights when I haven't had to.

Anon.

I learned law so well, the day I graduated I sued the college, won the case and got my tuition back.

Fred Allen, American comedian

#LAWS AND LAWYERS

… I don't think you can make a lawyer honest by an act of legislature. You've got to work on his conscience. And his lack of conscience is what makes him a lawyer.

Will Rogers, American humorist

One of the things I like most about lawyers is the big shock absorber they have strapped to their brains. Put it this way, if a lawyer's ego was hit by lightning, the lightning would be hospitalised.

Kathy Lette, *Altar Ego* (1998)

A town that cannot support one lawyer, can always support two.

Lyndon B. Johnson, President of the United States 1963–69

You've heard about the man who got the bill from his lawyer which said, 'For crossing the street to speak to you and discovering it was not you … twelve dollars.'

George S. Kaufman, American playwright and critic

Remember, if there had never been any lawyers, there would never have been any need for them.

>Anon.

Did you hear about the lawyer who was so clever he didn't bother to graduate? He just settled out of class.

>Anon.

I'm a criminal lawyer.
Thank you for being so frank.

>Anon.

I do not care to speak ill of any man behind his back, but I believe the gentleman is an attorney.

>Samuel Johnson, English writer

My definition of utter waste is a coachload of lawyers going over a cliff with three empty seats.

>Lamar Hunt, American sportsman and promoter

If you were stranded on a desert island with Osama Bin Laden, Saddam Hussein and a lawyer and you had a gun with only two bullets, what would you do?
I'd shoot the lawyer twice.

>Anon.

Q: What's the difference between a proud rooster and a lawyer?
A: The rooster clucks defiance...

>Anon.

If you see a lawyer on a bicycle, why shouldn't you swerve and hit him?
It might be your bicycle.
   Anon.

What's the difference between a lawyer and a catfish?
One is a scum-sucking bottom dweller and the other is a fish.
   Anon.

Why does California have the most lawyers and New Jersey the most toxic waste dumps?
Because New Jersey had first choice.
   Anon.

Talk is cheap, until you call a lawyer.
   Anon.

If a lawyer and a taxman were both drowning and you could only save one of them, would you go to lunch or just read the paper?
   Anon.

Why is it unethical for lawyers to have sex with their clients?
Because it means being billed twice for essentially the same service.
   Anon.

What's the difference between a lawyer and a bucket of dirt?
The bucket.
   Anon.

God bless lawyers. If we didn't have them, how would we ever get out of the trouble they got us into?

Anon.

Hell hath no fury like the lawyer of a woman scorned.

Anon.

I've got a brilliant lawyer. He can look at a contract and in less than a minute tell you whether it's oral or written.

Anon.

Old lawyers never die, they just lose their appeal.

Anon.

Q: What do you have when a lawyer is buried up to his neck in wet cement?
A: Not enough cement.

Anon.

Did you hear about the terrorist who hijacked a 747 full of lawyers? He threatened to release one every hour until his demands were met.

Anon.

Why Experiment on Animals With So Many Lawyers Out There?

Bumper sticker

Ninety-nine per cent of lawyers give the rest a bad name.

Anon.

A lawyer is a man who helps you get what's coming to him.
  Anon.

A lawyer is someone who prevents somebody else from getting your money.
  Anon.

See also #LAW, THE

#LAZINESS

Laziness is nothing more than the habit of resting before you get tired.
  Jules Renard, French author

It's impossible to enjoy idling thoroughly unless one has plenty of work to do.
  Jerome K. Jerome, *Idle Thoughts of an Idle Fellow* (1886)

You labourers are so lazy. You've been sitting there all day, doing absolutely nothing.
How do you know?
I've been sitting here watching you.
  Anon.

The boss found an employee asleep on the job so he woke him up. Coming to his senses, the employee said, 'Good heavens, can't a man even close his eyes for a few moments of prayer?'
  Anon.

I've stopped drinking coffee in the morning, because it keeps me awake for the rest of the day.

Sally Poplin, British humorous writer

I missed my nap today. I slept right through it.

Sally Poplin, British humorous writer

My uncle is so lazy ...
- Ever since he's been old enough to hold down a steady job, he hasn't.
- He hates mornings. He gets up at the crack of noon.
- I keep telling my uncle to learn a trade, so at least he'll know what sort of work he's out of!
- He did once think about getting a job. Then he decided that would be the coward's way out.
- I'll tell you how lazy he is – he's dating a pregnant woman!
- He's got a great way of starting the day: he goes back to bed.
- My uncle is very religious. He won't work if there's a Sunday in the week.
- My uncle does absolutely nothing around the house. Recently his wife had him searched for a socket. She wondered if maybe she had to plug him in!
- My uncle is very superstitious. He won't work in any week that has a Friday in it.
- My uncle was rejected by the army because he had a problem with his back. He couldn't get off it.
- No wonder my uncle doesn't work very often. He describes himself as a Coronation programme seller.

- One firm offered him a raise if he worked hard. He knew there was a catch there somewhere.
- He was born with a silver spoon in his mouth – and he hasn't stirred since.
- He's devised this great labour-saving device. It's called 'tomorrow'.
- He's got two desks in his office – one for each foot.
- He's so lazy, he won't even exercise discretion.
- He's so lazy, he even married a widow with five children.
- I don't think my uncle can be serious about getting a job. He says the only one he'll take is marriage guidance counsellor to the Pope.

Jerry Dennis, *Larry the Lazy Uncle* (2014)

Lazy? He used to ride his bike over cobblestones to knock the ash off his ciggie.

Les Dawson, *The Les Dawson Joke Book* (1979)

The laziest man I ever met put popcorn in his pancakes so they would turn over by themselves.

W. C. Fields, American actor and comedian

It is better to have loafed and lost than never to have loafed at all.

James Thurber, *Fables for Our Time* (1943)

He works eight hours a day and sleeps eight hours a day – the same eight hours.

Milton Berle, American actor and comedian

My husband has always felt that marriage and a career don't mix; that's why he's never worked.
Phyllis Diller, American comedian Hard work pays off in the future. Laziness pays off now.
Steven Wright, American comedian

#LEADERSHIP

First rule of leadership: everything is your fault.
Donald McEnery, *A Bug's Life* (1998)

A leader is a dealer in hope.
Napoleon Bonaparte, French military and political leader

Soldiers win battles but generals get the credit.
Napoleon Bonaparte, French military and political leader

It is an interesting question how much men would retain their relative rank if they were divested of their clothes.
David Henry Thoreau, American historian and philosopher

Leadership, like swimming, cannot be learned by reading about it.
Henry Minizberg, Canadian writer and educator

Every despot must have one disloyal subject to keep them sane.
George Bernard Shaw, Irish playwright

Look over your shoulder now and then to be sure someone's following you.

    Henry Gilmer, American writer

When you're getting kicked in the rear, it must mean you're
in front.

    Fulton J. Sheen, American bishop of the Roman Catholic
    Church

Charlatanism of some degree is indispensable to effective
leadership.

    Eric Hoffer, American moral philosopher

People should know what you stand for.
They should also know what you won't stand for.

    Mary H. Waldrip, English nurse

A mean streak is a very important quality of leadership.

    Charles E. Goodell, American lawyer and senator

You do not lead by hitting people over the head. That's
assault, not leadership.

    Dwight D. Eisenhower, President of the United States
    1953–61

I never give them hell. I just tell the truth and they think
it's hell.

    Harry S. Truman, President of the United States 1945–53

If you hit your pony over the nose at the outset of your acquaintance, he may not love you, but he will take a deep interest in your movements ever afterwards.

Rudyard Kipling, British poet

Leadership is the ability to get men to do what they don't want to do and like it.

Harry S. Truman, President of the United States 1945–53

It is a fine thing to command, even if it only be a herd of cattle.

Miguel de Cervantes, *Don Quixote* (1605)

The disdain that political leaders show the ordinary citizen is reciprocated.

Barry Sussman, American political analyst

Leadership is the ability to decide what is to be done and then to get others to want to do it.

Dwight D. Eisenhower, President of the United States 1953–61

It is amazing what you can accomplish if you do not care who gets the credit.

Harry S. Truman, President of the United States 1945–53

The task of the leader is to get his people from where they are to where they have not been.

Henry Kissinger, American diplomat

The greatest leaders throughout history have been notoriously poor followers.

Katheryn Collins, American businesswoman

If you're not afraid to face the music, you may someday lead the band.

David Frost, English journalist

The trouble with being a leader today is that you can't be sure if the people are following you or chasing you.

David Frost, English journalist

When the best leader's work is done, the people say, 'We did it ourselves.'

Lao-tzu, legendary philosopher of ancient China

It's a terrible thing when you look over your shoulder when you are trying to lead – and to find no one there.

Franklin D. Roosevelt, President of the United States
1933–45

We can't all be heroes because somebody has to sit on the curb and clap as they go by.

Will Rogers, American humorist

Only one man in a thousand is a leader of men – the other 999 follow women.

Groucho Marx, American comedian and actor

Either lead, follow or get out of the way.

Sign on Ted Turner's desk

We have leadership – there's just no followership.

George Danielson, US Congressman

A smile for a friend and a sneer for the world is the way to govern mankind.

Benjamin Disraeli, two-time British Prime Minister

Leadership involves finding a parade and getting in front of it.

John Naisbitt, American futurist and writer

I believe in benevolent dictatorship, provided I am the dictator.

Richard Branson, British business magnate

I must follow them. I am their leader.

Andrew Bonar Law, British Prime Minister 1922–23

#LUCK

A rabbit's foot may be lucky – but not for the original owner.

Anon.

For years he waited for Dame Fortune to come knocking on his door. Finally, someone did knock, but when he opened the door it was Dame Fortune's daughter, Miss Fortune.

Anon.

If I didn't have bad luck, I wouldn't have any luck at all.
  Anon.

Just my luck! When my ship came in, I was stuck at the airport!
  Max Kauffmann, American comedian

If you put the milk in your tea first, it's extremely unlucky. My great-aunt Clarice one day put the milk in first and over the course of the next fifty years, she lost all her teeth.
  Anon.

I'm very lucky. The only time I was ever up shit creek, I just happened to have a paddle with me.
  George Carlin, *Brain Droppings* (1997)

I believe in luck: how else can you explain the success of those you dislike?
  Jean Cocteau, French poet and novelist

I am a great believer in luck and I find the harder I work the more I have of it.
  Stephen Leacock, *Literary Lapses* (1910)

I broke a mirror in my house, which is supposed to be seven years' bad luck. My lawyer thinks he can get me five.
  Steven Wright, American comedian

M

#MANAGEMENT

Managing is like holding a dove in your hand. Squeeze too hard and you kill it; not hard enough and it flies away.

Tommy Lasorda, baseball manager

Managers are like cats in a litterbox. They instinctively shuffle things around to conceal what they've done.

Scott Adams, American cartoonist and creator of *Dilbert*

There are times when the best manager is like the little boy with the big dog, waiting to see where the dog wants to go so he can take him there.

Lee Iacocca, American businessman

There are only three types of manager: those who make things happen, those who watch things happen, and those who say, 'What happened?'

Anon.

The Five Golden Rules of Management
1. Delegating is a sign of weakness. Let someone else do it.
2. Creativity is great but plagiarism is faster.
3. If God had meant everyone to be a high flyer, he wouldn't have invented the ground.
4. If at first you do succeed, try to hide your astonishment.
5. If at first you *don't* succeed, redefine success.
   Anon.

The first myth of management is that it exists.
   Anon.

The successful man is the one who finds out what is the matter with his business before his competitors do.
   Roy L. Smith, American businessman

If at first you don't succeed, try management.
   Anon.

The secret of managing is to keep the guys who hate you away from the guys who are undecided.
   Casey Stengel, American Major League baseball outfielder and manager

Never tell people how to do things. Tell them what to do and they will surprise you with their ingenuity.
   George S. Patton, United States Army General

This is a story about four people named Everybody, Somebody, Anybody, and Nobody. There was an important job to be done and Everybody was sure that Somebody would do it. Anybody could have done it, but Nobody did it. Somebody got angry about that, because it was Everybody's job. Everybody thought Anybody could do it, but Nobody realised that Everybody wouldn't do it. It ended up that Everybody blamed Somebody when Nobody did what Anybody could have.

Anon.

See also #BOSSES

#MARKETING

Marketing is far too important to leave to the marketing department.

David Packard, founder of Hewlett Packard

Give a man a fish and he will eat for a day. Teach a man to fish and he will eat for a lifetime. Teach a man to create an artificial shortage of fish and he will eat steak.

Jay Leno, American television host

These are difficult days for automobile manufacturers; they're thinking up ways of making their products safer and new names to make them sound more dangerous.

Thomas La Mance, American wit

A new study says you idiots will believe anything that starts off with 'a new study says'.

Twitter, 2011

Without strategy, content is just stuff. And the world has enough stuff.

Pinterest, 2013

If Botticelli were alive today he'd be working for *Vogue*.

Peter Ustinov, English actor and writer

Master your Strengths, Outsource Your Weaknesses.

Ryan Kahn, American career coach

Had a look at the alligators. Just floating handbags, really.

Trevor Griffiths, English dramatist

Marketing is what you do when your product is no good.

Edwin Land, photographic pioneer

Many aspects of the writing life have changed since I published my first book, in the 1960s. It is more corporate, more driven by profits and marketing, and generally less congenial – but my day is the same: get out of bed, procrastinate, sit down at my desk, try to write something.

Paul Theroux, American novelist

The real axis of evil in America is the genius of our marketing and the gullibility of our people.

Bill Maher, *When You Ride Alone You Ride With Bin Laden: What the Government Should Be Telling Us to Help Fight the War on Terrorism* (2002)

I persuade, you educate, they manipulate.

Dr Allen Crawford, American wit

Marketing wants 'Mr Right' but Sales but wants 'Mr Right Now'.
Anon.

We have a strategic plan. It's called doing things.
Herb Kelleher, co-founder of Southwest Airlines

If the package doesn't say, 'New', these days, it better say, 'Seven cents off'.
Spencer Klaw, journalist and author

'I love being marketed to.' Said no one, ever.
Twitter, 2013

The market potential in China is one billion toothbrushes and two billion armpits.
Anon.

Here is a simple but powerful rule ... always give people more than they expect to get.
Nelson Boswell, American self-help author

See also #ADVERTISING

#MEETINGS

Rome did not create a great empire by having meetings. They did it by killing all those who opposed them.
Bumper sticker

Meetings ... are rather like cocktail parties. You don't want to go, but you're cross not to be asked.

Jilly Cooper, *How to Survive from Nine to Five* (1970)

Meetings are indispensable when you don't want to do anything.

John Kenneth Galbraith, Canadian economist

The Law of Triviality. Briefly stated, it means that the time spent on any item of the agenda will be in inverse proportion to the sum involved.

C. Northcote Parkinson, 'High Finance', *Parkinson's Law* (1957)

Meetings: A practical alternative to work.

Anon.

If you had to identify in one word the reason why the human race has not achieved and never will achieve its full potential, that word would be *meetings*.

Dave Barry, American author and columnist

Meetings are an addictive, highly self-indulgent activity that corporations and other large organisations habitually engage in only because they cannot actually masturbate.

Dave Barry, American author and columnist

See also #COMMITTEES

#MISTAKES

For maximum attention, nothing beats a good mistake.
Sally Poplin, British humorous writer

Show me a man who doesn't make mistakes and I'll show you a man who doesn't do anything.
Theodore Roosevelt, President of the United States 1901–09

The only real mistake is the one from which we learn nothing.
Henry Ford, American industrialist

Mistakes are part of the dues one pays for a full life.
Sophia Loren, Italian actress

It was when I found out I could make mistakes that I knew I was on to something.
Ornette Coleman, American composer and saxophonist

If you don't make mistakes, you're not working on hard enough problems. And that's a big mistake.
Frank Wilczek, American theoretical physicist and Nobel laureate

As long as the world is turning and spinning, we're gonna be dizzy and we're gonna make mistakes.
Mel Brooks, American director and comedian

#MISTAKES/FORECASTS/BUSINESS BLUNDERS

This 'telephone' has too many shortcomings to be seriously considered as a means of communication. The device is inherently of no value to us.

Western Union internal memo (1876)

Computers in the future may weigh no more than 1.5 tons.

Popular Mechanics (1949)

I think there is a world market for maybe five computers.

Thomas Watson, chairman of IBM

640K ought to be enough for anybody.

Bill Gates, co-founder of Microsoft

I have travelled the length and breadth of this country and talked with the best people, and I can assure you that data processing is a fad that won't last out the year.

The editor in charge of business books for Prentice Hall

But what ... is it good for?

Engineer at the Advanced Computing Systems Division of IBM, 1968, commenting on the microchip

There is no reason anyone would want a computer in their home.

Ken Olson, president, chairman and founder of Digital Equipment Corp.

The wireless music box has no imaginable commercial value. Who would pay for a message sent to nobody in particular?

David Sarnoff's associates in response to his urgings for investment in the radio in the 1920s

The concept is interesting and well-formed, but in order to earn better than a 'C', the idea must be feasible.

A Yale University management professor in response to Fred Smith's paper proposing reliable overnight delivery service. (Smith went on to found Federal Express Corp.)

Who the hell wants to hear actors talk?

H. M. Warner, co-founder of Warner Brothers, 1927

I'm just glad it'll be Clark Gable who's falling on his face and not Gary Cooper.

Gary Cooper on his decision not to take the leading role in *Gone With The Wind*

We don't like their sound, and guitar music is on the way out.

Decca Recording Co. rejecting The Beatles in 1962

Heavier-than-air flying machines are impossible.

Lord Kelvin, President of the Royal Society 1890–95

Professor [Robert] Goddard does not know the relation between action and reaction and the need to have something better than a vacuum against which to react. He seems to lack the basic knowledge ladled out daily in high schools.

New York Times editorial about Robert Goddard's revolutionary rocket work (1921)

Airplanes are interesting toys but of no military value.
  Marshal Ferdinand Foch, Professor of Strategy, Ecole
  Supérieure de Guerre

Louis Pasteur's theory of germs is ridiculous fiction.
  Pierre Pachet, Professor of Physiology at Toulouse, 1872

Everything that can be invented has been invented.
  Charles H. Duell, United States Office of Patents commissioner, 1899

See also #FAILURES

#MONEY

Making money is the by-product not the goal.
  Randy D. Marsh, American businessman

The only bad thing about my seven-figure salary is that it
includes a decimal point.
  Facebook, 2011

Money is the fruit of evil as often as the root of it.
  Henry Fielding, English novelist and dramatist

Sometimes one pays most for the things one gets for nothing.
  Albert Einstein, German theoretical physicist

We all know how the size of sums of money appears to vary in a remarkable way according as they are being paid in or paid out.

Julian Huxley, *Essays of a Biologist* (1923)

Inflation hasn't ruined everything. A dime can still be used as a screwdriver.

H. Jackson Brown, Jr, *P. S. I Love You* (1990)

I cannot afford to waste my time making money.

Louis Agassiz, Swiss biologist and geologist

This planet has – or rather had – a problem, which was this: most of the people living on it were unhappy for pretty much of the time. Many solutions were suggested for this problem, but most of these were largely concerned with the movements of small green pieces of paper, which is odd because on the whole it wasn't the small green pieces of paper that were unhappy.

Douglas Adams, British comedy writer

There are a handful of people whom money won't spoil, and we count ourselves among them.

Mignon McLaughlin, American journalist

There are several ways in which to apportion the family income, all of them unsatisfactory.

Robert Benchley, American wit

Money is much more exciting than anything it buys.
  Mignon McLaughlin, *The Second Neurotic's Notebook*
  (1966)

Money isn't everything. Sometimes it isn't even enough.
  Anon.

If you had your life to live all over again, you'd need lots
of money.
  Jackie Mason, American comedian

That money talks,
I can't deny.
I heard it once –
It said, 'Goodbye.'
  Richard Armour, poet

I have never been in any situation where having money
made it worse.
  Clinton Jones, American footballer

Never underestimate the effectiveness of a straight cash bribe.
  Claud Cockburn, British journalist

Money often costs too much.
  Ralph Waldo Emerson, American essayist and poet

I never refuse money. I come from a family where it was
considered unlucky to refuse money.
  Patrick Kavanagh, Irish wit

If you would only know what the Lord God thinks of money, you only have to look at those to whom he gives it.
  Maurice Baring, British banker

All I ask is a chance to prove that money can't make me happy.
  Spike Milligan, British comedian

Money is just what we use to keep tally.
  Henry Ford, American industrialist

Money is the only true aristocracy.
  Victor Lewis-Smith, TV and restaurant critic

Money is better than poverty, if only for financial reasons.
  Woody Allen, *Without Feathers* (1972)

Can money make your hands get rough,
As washing dishes does?
Can money make you smell the way
That cooking fishes does?
It may buy you gems and fancy clothes
And juicy steaks to carve,
But it cannot build your character
Or teach you how to starve!
... Money *isn't* everything
As long as you have dough!
  Oscar Hammerstein II, 'Money isn't Everything', *Allegro* (1947)

All right, so I like spending money! But name one other extravagance!

Max Kauffmann, American comedian

Money can't buy friends but you can get a better class of enemy.

Spike Milligan, *Puckoon* (1963)

The great rule is not to talk about money with people who have much more or much less than you.

Katharine Whitehorn, British journalist

I don't want money. It is only people who pay their bills who want that, and I never pay mine.

Oscar Wilde, *The Picture of Dorian Gray* (1890)

Money can't buy you love – but it certainly puts you in a wonderful bargaining position.

Harrison Baker

Money isn't everything, but it sure keeps you in touch with your children.

J. Paul Getty, American industrialist

Money is the great equaliser. Money takes away all your faults. Money will turn a bald spot into a part.

Chris Rock, *Politically Incorrect*, 1994

Money, it turned out, was exactly like sex. You thought of nothing else if you didn't have it and thought of other things if you did.

James Baldwin, American novelist

Money is something you got to make in case you don't die.

Max Asnas, Russian-American restaurateur

The chief value of money lies in the fact that one lives in a world in which it is overestimated.

H. L. Mencken, American journalist

Money is like a sixth sense – and you can't make use of the other five without it.

W. Somerset Maugham, English novelist

Money is a stupid measure of achievement, but unfortunately it is the only universal measure we have.

Charles Steinmetz, American electrical engineer

There was a time when a fool and his money were soon parted, but now it happens to everybody.

Adlai Stevenson, American politician

The darkest hour of any man's life is when he sits down to plan how to make money without earning it.

Horace Greeley, American journalist and politician

See also #BANKS AND BANKING, #BUDGETS, #CREDIT, #DEBT, #ECONOMICS, #TAXATION, #WEALTH

N

#NEGOTIATIONS

When a man tells me he's going to put all his cards on the table, I always look up his sleeve.

Lord Hore-Belisha, British Secretary of State for War
1937–40

#NEPOTISM

This is my son, who's just joined the company. He's going to start at the bottom for a few days.

Anon.

When I say he's a born executive, I mean his father owns the business.
When it comes to having qualifications, it's hard to beat having a father who owns the company.

Jerry Dennis, British comedian

I made my money the old-fashioned way. I inherited it.
My boss had to do it the hard way. He had to be nice to
his father.

Anon.

Our company is one big happy family. Mainly because I
only give jobs to my relatives.

Max Kauffmann, American comedian

Nobody talks more of free enterprise and competition and
of the best man winning than the man who inherited his
father's store or farm.

C. Wright Mills, American sociologist

O

#OFFICE, THE

A memorandum is written not to inform the reader but to protect the writer.

Dean Acheson, American statesman

If people don't wish to discuss the cruel existential futility of all human endeavour they shouldn't say 'Good morning' in the first place.

Twitter, 2013

I yield to no one in my admiration for the office as a social centre but it's no place to actually get any work done.

Katharine Whitehorn, British journalist

Boss (*to Departmental Head*): How many people work in your office?

Dept. Head: About half of them, sir.

Gyles Brandreth, *1,000 Jokes: The Greatest Joke Book Ever Known* (1980)

A secretary is someone you pay to learn to type while she looks for a husband.

    Anon.

A secretary is not a thing
Wound by key, pulled by string.
Her pad is to write in,
And not spend the night in,
If that's what you plan to enjoy.
No!

    Frank Loesser, 'A Secretary is Not a Toy', *How to Succeed in Business without Really Trying* (1961)

Your face is a company face.
It smiles at executives then goes back in place.
The company furniture?
Oh, it suits me fine.
The company letterhead?
A valentine.
Anything you're against?
Unemployment.

    Frank Loesser, 'The Company Way', *How to Succeed in Business without Really Trying* (1961)

An office is not a tea-bar, matrimonial bureau, betting shop, reading room, fashion house or smoking lounge, but a place where paperwork necessary to good management is originated and eventually filed.

    Keith Waterhouse, *The Passing of the Third-floor Buck* (1974)

A man who has no office to go to – I don't care who he is – is a trial of which you can have no conception.

George Bernard Shaw, Irish playwright

Yesterday I got my tie stuck in the fax machine. Next thing I knew, I was in Los Angeles.

Anon.

Stress Is Your Body's Way Of Saying You Haven't Worked Enough Unpaid Overtime.

Scott Adams, American cartoonist and creator of *Dilbert*

Businessman on phone: 'Miss Bremmer, get me whatever coast I'm not on.'

Bob Mankoff, American cartoonist

If your desk isn't cluttered, you're probably not doing your job.

Harold S. Geneen, American businessman and President of ITT Corporation

#OFFICE POSTERS

- Two days without a human rights violation!
- The beatings will continue until morale improves.
- Pride, commitment, teamwork – words we use to get you to work for free.
- Aim low, reach your goals, avoid disappointment.
- Hang in there, retirement is only thirty years away!
- To err is human; to forgive is not company policy.

- Be punctual, be loyal, and above all, never forget that 'Manager' is an anagram for 'Complete and Total Bastard'!
- If the boss calls, get his name.

The Six Stages of Production
1. Wild Enthusiasm
2. Total Confusion
3. Utter Despair
4. Search for the Guilty
5. Persecution of the Innocent
6. Promotion of the Incompetent

#OIL

The price of petrol seems out of control.
Today a friend of mine did something smart. He bought a gallon as an investment.

Petrol is getting so expensive people are buying it by the half litre.

There have been some wild ideas for reducing oil prices – for instance, one think tank has suggested making all roads downhill.

Another expert suggested cheaper self-service at petrol stations if you pump and refine the oil yourself.

And did you notice that the first prize in the National Lottery this week is five gallons of unleaded?

'Drill for oil? You mean drill into the ground to try and find oil? You're crazy.'
   The response to Edwin L. Drake's pioneering project to
   drill for oil in 1859 from the drillers

#OPPORTUNITY

Every exit is an entrance somewhere else.
   Tom Stoppard, playwright

I despise making the most of one's time. Half the pleasures of life consist of the opportunities one has neglected.
   Oliver Wendell Holmes, Jr, American jurist

The reason so many people never get anywhere in life is because, when opportunity knocks, they are out in the back yard looking for four-leaf clovers.
   Walter Chrysler, founder of the Chrysler Corporation

If opportunity doesn't knock, build a door.
   Milton Berle, American comedian

Next to knowing when to seize an opportunity, the most important thing in life is to know when to forgo an advantage.
   Benjamin Disraeli, two-time British Prime Minister

We are confronted with insurmountable opportunities.

> Walt Kelly, American animator and cartoonist

Summing up, it is clear the future holds great opportunities. It also holds pitfalls. The trick will be to avoid the pitfalls, seize the opportunities, and get back home by six o'clock.

> Woody Allen, 'My Speech to the Graduates', *Side Effects* (1980)

#OPTIMISM AND PESSIMISM

An optimist is a man who starts a crossword puzzle with a fountain pen.

> Anon.

Optimism is the content of small men in high places.

> F. Scott Fitzgerald, *The Crack-up* (1945)

An optimist is a man who gets married at eighty-five and then buys a house near a school.

> Anon.

He's the eternal optimist. If he fell out of a window on the fortieth floor, as he passed the twentieth he'd still be saying, 'So far, so good.'

> Anon.

Never borrow money from an optimist. He always expects to get it back.

> Anon.

You've got a flat tyre.
Yes, but only at the bottom.
  Anon.

An optimist is a guy that has never had much experience.
  Don Marquis, 'Certain Maxims of Archy', *Archy and
  Mehitabel* (1927)

I'm an optimist, but I'm an optimist who carries a raincoat.
  Harold Wilson, two-time British Prime Minister

The optimist proclaims that we live in the best of all possible worlds; and the pessimist fears this is true.
  James Branch Cabell, *The Silver Stallion* (1926)

O, merry is the optimist,
With the troops of courage leaguing
But a dour trend
In any friend
Is somehow less fatiguing.
  Phyllis McGinley, 'Song against Sweetness and Light', *A
  Pocketful of Wry* (1940)

Twixt the optimist and the pessimist
The difference is droll:
The optimist sees the doughnut
But the pessimist sees the hole.
  McLandburgh Wilson, American writer

A pessimist is someone who sees a cloud in every silver lining.

Anon.

Life is divided into the horrible and the miserable.

Woody Allen and Marshall Brickman, *Annie Hall* (1977)

There are bad times just around the corner,
There are dark clouds hurtling through the sky
And it's no good whining
About a silver lining
For we know from experience that they won't roll by,
With a scowl and a frown
We'll keep our peckers down
And prepare for depression and doom and dread,
We're going to unpack our troubles from our old kit bag
And wait until we drop down dead.

Noël Coward, 'There are Bad Times just Around the Corner', *Globe Revue* (1952)

A pessimist is a man who has been compelled to live with an optimist.

Elbert Hubbard, *The Notebook* (1927)

Things are going to get a lot worse before they get worse.

Lily Tomlin, American comedian

The nice part about being a pessimist is that you are constantly being proven right or pleasantly surprised.

George Will, American political commentator

A pessimist is an optimist on his way home from the racetrack.

Anon.

An optimist is someone who sees the opportunity in every catastrophe; a pessimist is someone who sees the catastrophe in every opportunity.

Anon.

What's the difference between an optimist and a pessimist? An optimist invented the aeroplane; a pessimist invented the seat belts.

Anon.

There is no sadder sight than a young pessimist, except an old optimist.

Mark Twain, American author

P

#PERSEVERANCE

Consider the postage stamp: its usefulness consists in the ability to stick to one thing till it gets there.

Josh Billings, American wit

It's not that I'm so smart, it's just that I stay with problems longer.

Albert Einstein, German theoretical physicist

I may not be there yet, but I'm closer than I was yesterday.

Anon.

I could never finish anything, but now I …

Anon.

Never give up and never give in.

Hubert Humphrey, Vice-President of the United States 1965–69

Perseverance: a lowly virtue whereby mediocrity achieves an inglorious success.

Ambrose Bierce, *The Devil's Dictionary* (1911)

#PHILANTHROPY

We cannot live only for ourselves. A thousand fibres connect us with our fellow men.

Herman Melville, American novelist

Our charity begins at home – and mostly ends where it begins.

Horace Smith, American inventor and manufacturer

The entire population of the universe, with one trifling exception, is composed of others.

John Andrew Holmes, American writer

What do we live for if not to make life less difficult for each other?

George Eliot, English novelist

Provision for others is a fundamental responsibility of human life.

Woodrow Wilson, President of the United States 1913–21

Giving away a fortune is taking Christianity too far.

Charlotte Bingham, English novelist

Philanthropy ... simply the refuge of people who wish to annoy their fellow creatures.

Oscar Wilde, Irish playwright

An idealist is someone who helps other people to be prosperous.

Henry Ford, American industrialist

You can be social-minded without being a socialist.

Charles E. Wilson, United States Secretary of Defence
1953–57

The greatest good you can do for another is not just to share your riches, but to reveal to him his own.

Benjamin Disraeli, two-time British Prime Minister

The gods sent not,
Corn for the rich men only.

William Shakespeare, *Coriolanus* (c. 1608)

Paul Newman became one of the most famous social entre-preneurs when he started selling salad dressing and donat-ing the profits to charitable causes.
He said, 'Our motto was, "Shameless exploitation in pursuit of the common good."'
Did you see that Microsoft's Bill Gates has donated a million pounds to the NSPCC?
And all *they've* got to do in return is rename themselves MSNSPCC.

Anon.

The man who dies rich, dies disgraced.

Andrew Carnegie, Scottish-American industrialist

You know what they say: Give a man a fish and he can eat for a day. But teach a man how to fish and he'll be dead of mercury poisoning within three years.

Charles Haas, American screenwriter, actor and novelist

Time and money spent in helping men to do more for themselves is far better than mere giving.

Henry Ford, American industrialist

Everybody lives for something better to come.

Maxim Gorky, Russian writer

Hope! Of all the ills that men endure, the only cheap and universal cure.

Abraham Cowley, seventeenth-century English poet

If it were not for hopes,
The heart would break.

Thomas Fuller, seventeenth-century British physician

#POLITICS

George Orwell would not blow his nose without moralising about the conditions in the handkerchief industry.

Cyril Connolly, English commentator

See also #POWER

#POWER

A friend in power is a friend lost.
  Henry Adams, *The Education of Henry Adams* (1906)

It is certainly more agreeable to have power to give than to receive.
  Winston Churchill, British statesman and orator

Power is the ultimate aphrodisiac.
  Henry Kissinger, American diplomat

Power corrupts, but lack of power corrupts absolutely.
  Adlai Stevenson, American politician

See also #POLITICS

#PROBLEMS

What on earth would a man do with himself if something didn't stand in his way?
  H. G. Wells, English science fiction writer

I put my problems down to three things: women, money – and both those two.
  Anon.

When you're up to your armpits in alligators, it's hard to remember to drain the swamp.
  Ronald Reagan, President of the United States 1981–89

The problems of the world today are so complex that even teenagers don't have the answer.

Anon.

There is always an easy solution to every human problem – neat, plausible and wrong.

H. L. Mencken, American journalist

The way I look at it, if you want the rainbow, you gotta put up with the rain.

Dolly Parton, American singer-songwriter

No problem is so big or so complicated that it can't be run away from!

Charles M. Schulz, American cartoonist

The chief cause of problems is solutions.

Eric Sevareid, American television reporter

#PROFESSIONS

A profession is something you study for years to get into, then work for the rest of your life trying to earn enough money to get out of.

Sally Poplin, British humorous writer

Professionals built the *Titanic*; amateurs built the Ark.

Anon.

Incomprehensible jargon is the hallmark of a profession.

Kingman Brewster, American educator and diplomat

The best augury of a man's success in his profession is that he thinks it the finest in the world.

George Eliot, English novelist

#PUNCTUALITY

Punctuality is the art of guessing correctly how late the other party is going to be.

American proverb

The only way of catching a train I ever discovered is to miss the train before.

G. K. Chesterton, English writer

I have noticed that the people who are late are often so much jollier than the people who have to wait for them.

E. V. Lucas, *Reading, Writing and Remembering* (1932)

People count up the faults of those who keep them waiting.

French proverb

I've been on a calendar, but never on time.

Marilyn Monroe, American actress and singer

Someday is not a day of the week.
  Anon.

Being early is an unpardonable sin. If you are early, you'll witness the last-minute confusion and panic that always attend making anything seem effortlessly gracious. Looking in on this scene is almost as rude as asking someone where he got his face-lift.
  P. J. O'Rourke, *Modern Manners* (1983)

If a thing is worth doing, it's worth doing late.
  Freddie Oliver, English comedian

The trouble with being punctual is that there's nobody there to appreciate it.
  Harold Rome, American composer and lyricist

Punctuality is the virtue of the bored.
  Evelyn Waugh, *Diaries* (1976)

He was always late on principle, his principle being that punctuality is the thief of time.
  Oscar Wilde, *The Picture of Dorian Gray* (1890)

If it weren't for the last minute, nothing would ever get done.
  Anon.

R

#RESEARCH

Research is the process of going up alleys to see if they're blind.
Marston Bates, American zoologist

No amount of experimentation can ever prove me right; a single experiment can prove me wrong.
Albert Einstein, German theoretical physicist

The way to do research is to attack the facts at the point of greatest astonishment.
Celia Green, British writer

Research shows that when someone shouts, 'Oh no he didn't!', he in fact did.
Facebook, 2011

Successful research impedes further successful researches.
Keith J. Pendred, scientist

We have paralysis by analysis.

Anon.

Negative results are just what I want. They're just as valuable to me as positive results. I can never find the thing that does the job best until I find the ones that don't.

Thomas Edison, American inventor and scientist

#RETIREMENT

Retirement means twice as much husband on half as much money.

Anon.

Retirement at sixty-five is ridiculous. When I was sixty-five, I still had pimples.

George Burns, American comedian

[Retirement] … one sure way of shortening life.

Frank Conklin, American wit

Your mother is so dumb, when her boss told her to retire, she went out and bought four Michelins.

Anon.

You're sixty-five today – and it's the first day of the rest of your life savings!

Anon.

When a man retires and time is no longer a matter of urgent importance, his colleagues generally present him with a watch.

R. C. Sherriff, English writer

If my calculations are correct, I can retire about five years after I die.

Tumblr, 2013

I've been attending lots of seminars in my retirement. They're called naps.

Merri Brownworth, American wit

It's nice to get out of the rat race, but you have to learn to get along with less cheese.

Gene Perret, American joke writer

I'm retired – goodbye tension, hello pension!

Anon.

There are some who start their retirement long before they stop working.

Robert Half, American businessman

I enjoy waking up and not having to go to work. So I do it three or four times a day.

Gene Perret, American joke writer

Youth would be an ideal state if it came a little later in life.

Herbert Asquith, British Prime Minister 1908–16

First you forget names; then you forget faces; then you forget to zip up your fly; and then you forget to unzip your fly.

Branch Rickey, Major League Baseball executive

Retirement kills more people than hard work ever did.

Malcolm S. Forbes, American publisher

Six months ago 541,000 people obeyed a single command I gave. Today it's even difficult to get a plumber to do what I want.

Herman Norman Schwarzkopf, United States Army
general, after retirement

I married him for better or worse, but not for lunch.

Hazel Weiss, after her husband, George Weiss, retired as
general manager of the New York Yankees

At his retirement ceremony the boss told him, 'The way we see it, we're not so much losing a worker as gaining a parking space.'

Anon.

Look before you leap. Before you retire, stay home for a week and watch daytime television.

Anon.

See also #GOLF, #HUMAN RESOURCES,
#UNEMPLOYMENT

S

#SALES AND SELLING

First salesman: I made some very valuable contacts today.
Second salesman: I didn't get any orders either.

Anon.

January cover: If You Don't Buy This Magazine, We'll Kill This Dog.

February editorial page: Remember it? The dog that was going to be killed if you didn't buy the issue? You people are really incredible. You had us kill that sweet pooch. And don't for a minute go blaming us. We held the gun, but you sure as hell pulled the trigger ... though there are those among you who did buy three or four issues to take up whatever slack existed. Those people are to be commended. But it wasn't enough. It was for everyone to pull his or her share. And you didn't.

National Lampoon (1973)

A salesman has got to dream, boy, it comes with the territory.

Arthur Miller, *Death of a Salesman* (1949)

Is he a good salesman? He could sell underarm deodorant to the Venus de Milo.

Anon.

The person who agrees with everything you say either isn't paying attention or else plans to sell you something.

Sam Ewing, American author

Inequality of knowledge is the key to a sale.

Deil O. Gustafson, American real estate executive

People will buy anything that's 'one to a customer'.

Sinclair Lewis, American novelist and playwright

He calls himself an independent salesman. He takes orders from no one.

Max Kauffmann, American comedian

To sell something, tell a woman it's a bargain; tell a man it's deductible.

Earl Wilson, newspaper columnist

See also #CUSTOMERS, #SHOPS AND SHOPPING

#SCIENCE AND SCIENTISTS

According to a study published by *Nature* magazine, queen bees are born with the ability to give accurate directions. Unfortunately the male bees refuse to ask for them.

Anon.

It is a good idea for a research scientist to discard a pet hypothesis every day before breakfast.

Konrad Lorenz, zoologist

The universe is full of magical things patiently waiting for our wits to grow sharper.

Eden Philpotts, English poet

Science is a lot of little guys in tweed suits cutting up frogs on foundation grants.

Woody Allen, actor and writer

If rocket scientists are so smart, why do they all count backwards?

Anon.

I've always wanted to ask a scientist, how do they get Teflon to stick to frying pans?

Anon.

Modern science was largely conceived of as an answer to the servant problem and ... is generally practiced by those who lack a flair for conversation.

Fran Lebowitz, *Metropolitan Life* (1978)

The latest news from NASA is that Mars was at one time covered with water, which means that it could have supported life.
Of course, water doesn't necessarily mean intelligent life – as anyone who watched *Celebrity Love Island* will know.

Anon.

I see that the Chinese have cancelled plans to put a man on the moon.

The thinking behind it is that they only deliver within a 100,000-mile radius.

Anon.

The essence of science: ask an impertinent question and you are on the way to a pertinent answer.

Jacob Bronowski, scientist, poet and inventor

I met a boffin last year who told me he'd invented a liquid that would dissolve anything.

It'll be on the market just as soon as he can find something to keep it in.

Anon.

Science is always wrong. It never solves a problem without creating ten more.

George Bernard Shaw, Irish playwright

A drug is a substance that when injected into a guinea pig produces a scientific paper.

Anon.

Scientists – a crowd that when it comes to style and dash makes the general public look like the Bloomsbury set.

Fran Lebowitz, *Metropolitan Life* (1978)

The scientific theory I like best is that the rings of Saturn are composed entirely of lost airline luggage.

Jerry Dennis, British comedian

To mistrust science and deny the validity of the scientific method is to resign your job as a human. You'd better go look for work as a plant or wild animal.

P. J. O'Rourke, *Parliament of Whores* (1991)

Although this may seem a paradox, all exact science is dominated by the idea of approximation. When a man tells you that he knows the exact truth about anything, you are safe in inferring that he is an inexact man.

Bertrand Russell, British philosopher

Ever wondered what the speed of lightning would be if it didn't zigzag?

Anon.

Two hydrogen atoms walk into a bar. The first one says, 'Oh, no, I've lost an electron!' The other one says, 'Are you sure?' The first one says, 'I'm positive!'

Anon.

My ignorance of science is such that if anyone mentioned copper nitrate, I should think he was talking about policemen's overtime.

Donald Coggan, Archbishop of Canterbury 1974–80

If it squirms, it's biology; if it stinks, it's chemistry; if it doesn't work, it's physics and if you can't understand it, it's mathematics.

Magnus Pyke, British scientist and broadcaster

The formula for water is H_2O. Is the formula for an ice cube H_2O squared?

Lily Tomlin, American comedian

The mouse is an animal which, killed in sufficient numbers under carefully controlled conditions, will produce a PhD thesis.

The Journal of Irreproducible Results

See also #TECHNOLOGY

#SHOPS AND SHOPPING

To open a shop is easy; to keep it open is an art.

Confucius, Chinese politician and philosopher

When buyers don't fall for prices, prices must fall for buyers.

Anon.

Shopping is a woman thing. It's a contact sport like football. Women enjoy the scrimmage, the noisy crowds, the danger of being trampled to death, and the ecstasy of the purchase.

Erma Bombeck, American humorist

Whoever determined that a one-inch candy bar should be called 'fun sized' should really re-evaluate their standards for entertainment.

Facebook, 2013

Still amazed that The Bible was so specific in forbidding shops with 280 square metres of floor space to open for over six hours on a Sunday.

Twitter, 2013

When women are depressed, they eat or go shopping. Men invade another country. It's a whole different way of thinking.

Elayne Boosler, American comedian

Buying something on sale is a very special feeling. In fact, the less I pay for something, the more it is worth to me. I have a dress that I paid so little for that I am afraid to wear it. I could spill something on it, and then how would I replace it for that amount of money?

Rita Rudner, American comedian

We used to build civilizations. Now we build shopping malls.

Bill Bryson, American travel writer

A bargain is something you can't use at a price you can't resist.

Franklin P. Jones, American journalist and wit

I love to go shopping. I love to freak out salespeople. They ask me if they can help me, and I say, 'Have you got anything I'd like?' Then they ask me what size I need, and I say, 'Extra medium.'

Steven Wright, American comedian

The odds of going to the store for a loaf of bread and coming
out with only a loaf of bread are three billion to one.
  Erma Bombeck, American humorist

I've been shopping all my life and still have nothing to wear.
  Sally Poplin, British humorous writer

A bargain ain't a bargain unless it's something you need.
  Sidney Carroll, American screenwriter

Anyone who believes the competitive spirit in America is
dead has never been in a supermarket when the cashier
opens another checkout line.
  Ann Landers, American advice columnist

Only one shopping day left till tomorrow!
  Anon.

I went to a general store but they wouldn't let me buy
anything specific.
  Steven Wright, American comedian

If the shoe fits, buy it in every colour!
  Sally Poplin, British humorous writer

Shopping: The fine art of acquiring things you don't need
with money you don't have.
  Anon.

The woman just ahead of you at the supermarket checkout has all the delectable groceries you didn't even know they carried.

Mignon McLaughlin, American journalist

Once again, we come to the Holiday Season, a deeply religious time that each of us observes, in his own way, by going to the mall of his choice.

Dave Barry, American author and columnist

The only reason a great many American families don't own an elephant is that they have never been offered an elephant for a dollar down and easy weekly payments.

Mad Magazine

Oh, for the good old days when people would stop Christmas shopping when they ran out of money.

Anon.

See also #SALES AND SELLING

#SLOGANS

We put the 'k' in 'kwality'.

Anon.

Bonzo Snax – the dog food so good it doesn't need a slogan.

Poster, Exeter

Men are from Earth, Women are from Earth. Deal with it.
   T-shirt slogan, Florida

We repair what your husband fixed.
   Sign on plumber's truck, New York

Nobody knows the truffles we've seen.
   Sign on Nevada City Truffles, Nevada City, California

If you don't get it, you don't get it.
   Ad for the *Washington Post*

There Are Some Things Money Can't Buy.
For Everything Else, There's MasterCard.
   Advertising slogan created by McCann Erickson

See also #ADVERTISING

#SMARTPHONES

I'm getting tired of having to write 'Sent from my iPhone' at the end of all my e-mails. Maybe I should just get an iPhone.
   Facebook, 2014

I don't have a smartphone, I have a phone that shows potential but doesn't apply itself.
   Facebook, 2011

I miss being able to slam my phone down when I hang up on somebody. Violently pressing 'end call' just doesn't do it for me.

Facebook, 2010

Hey smartphone owners! That blurred bit just off the edge of the screen is called life.

Facebook, 2013

#SMOKING

It's always been my rule never to smoke when asleep and never to refrain when awake.

Mark Twain, American author

As ye smoke, so shall ye reek.

Anon., *Reader's Digest*

I read in the *Reader's Digest* that cigarettes are bad for you. So I had to give up reading the *Reader's Digest*.

Anon.

I never smoked a cigarette until I was nine.

W. C. Fields, American actor and comedian

Smoking is, if not my life, then at least my hobby. I love to smoke. Smoking is fun. Smoking is cool. Smoking is, as far as I am concerned, the entire point of being an adult.

Fran Lebowitz, *Social Studies* (1981)

Smoking is very bad for you and should only be done because it looks so good. People who don't smoke have a terrible time finding something polite to do with their lips.

P. J. O'Rourke, *Modern Manners* (1983)

I've been smoking for thirty years now and there's nothing wrong with my lung.

Freddie Starr, British comedian

Usually we trust that nature has a master plan. But what was it she expected us to do with tobacco?

Bill Vaughan, American columnist

Thank You For Holding Your Breath While I Smoke

T-shirt slogan, Miami

I quit smoking. I feel better, I smell better and it's safer to drink from old beer cans around the house.

Roseanne Barr, American actress and comedian

People are so rude to smokers. You'd think they'd try to be nicer to people who are dying.

Roseanne Barr, American actress and comedian

I'm not really a heavy smoker any more. I only get through two lighters a day now.

Bill Hicks, American stand-up

#SOCIALISM

The function of socialism is to raise suffering to a higher level.
Norman Mailer, American novelist and essayist

As far as socialism means anything, it must be about the wider distribution of smoked salmon and caviar.
Richard Marsh, Labour Cabinet Minister

As with the Christian religion, the worst advertisement for socialism is its adherents.
George Orwell, *The Road to Wigan Pier* (1937)

The typical socialist ... a prim little man with a white-collar job, usually a secret teetotaller and often with vegetarian leanings.
George Orwell, *The Road to Wigan Pier* (1937)

We should have had socialism already, but for the socialists.
George Bernard Shaw, Irish playwright

Many people consider the things which government does for them as social progress, but they consider the things government does for others as socialism.
Earl Warren, Chief Justice of the United States 1953–69

At one time socialism might have been a good idea. Its inspiration, in those days, was generous and humane. Nowadays, it can appeal only to those whose social maladjustment might otherwise push them into the criminal classes, or whose intellectual inadequacies make them hungry for a dogmatic system in which they can hide their inability to think for themselves.

Auberon Waugh, *Spectator* (1984)

We'll find it very difficult to explain to the voters that simply by taking over Marks & Spencer we can make it as efficient as the Co-op.

Harold Wilson, two-time British Prime Minister

All animals are equal, but some animals are more equal than others.

George Orwell, *Animal Farm* (1945)

This list has been limited to members and cohorts of the Clinton administration, those simps and ninnies, lava-lamp liberals and condo pinks, spoiled twerps, wiffen-poofs, ratchet-jawed purveyors of monkey doodle and baked wind, piddlers upon merit, beggars at the door of accomplishment, thieves of livelihood, envy-coddling tax lice applauding themselves for their magnaminity with the money of others, their nose in virtue's bum.

P. J. O'Rourke, *The Enemies List* (1996)

Once the government has embarked upon a course of making all things fair, where is it to stop? Will tall people have to walk around on their knees? Will fat people be strapped to helium balloons? Will attractive people be made to wear ridiculous haircuts?

P. J. O'Rourke, *The Enemies List* (1996)

'Rabbi, can one build socialism in one country?'
'Yes, my son, but one must live in another.'

Anon.

Heckler: What about the workers' wages?
Candidate: When my party comes to power, workers' wages will be doubled!
Heckler: And what about the whores and tarts who defile our streets?
Candidate: My friend, when my party comes to power they will be driven underground.
Heckler: There you go again. Favouring the bloody miners!

Ian Aitken, *Guardian*

George: Fabled names in the annals of the New Left. All with monosyllabic names ... Stan, Mike, Les, Norm. As if to have two syllables in one's name were an indication of social pretension.

Alan Bennett, *Getting On* (1971)

See also #CAPITALISM, #TRADE UNIONS

#SPEAKERS AND SPEECHES

Tell them what you're going to tell them, tell them, then tell them what you told them.

Anonymous advice

An after-dinner speech should be like a lady's dress: long enough to cover the subject and short enough to be interesting.

    Anon.

You know what they say, all work and no plagiarism makes a dull speech.

    Anon.

The best way to stay awake during an after-dinner speech is to give it.

    Freddie Oliver, English comedian

Speak when you are angry and you will make the best speech you will ever regret.

    Ambrose Bierce, American satirist and critic

He's a man who is never lost for a few appropriated words.

    Anon.

Speeches are like steer horns – a point here, a point there and a lot of bull in between.

    Liberty

They said you can speak on just about anything and you don't have to be witty or intellectual. Just be yourself.

    A. Maurice Myers, CEO of Yellow Corp, on the host's
    guidance for his speech

I stand up when he nudges me. I sit down when they pull my coat.

Ernest Bevin, British statesman and politician

I do not object to people looking at their watches when I am speaking – but I strongly object when they start shaking them to make certain they are still going.

Lord Birkett, MP and lawyer

I feel like Zsa Zsa Gabor's fifth husband. I know what I'm supposed to do but I don't know if I can make it interesting.

Al Gore, Vice-President of the United States 1993–2001

If I am to speak for ten minutes, I need a week for preparation; if fifteen minutes three days; if half an hour, two days, if an hour I am ready now.

Woodrow Wilson, President of the United States 1913–21

Some microphones work great as long as you blow into them. So you stand there like an idiot blowing and saying, 'Are we on? Can you hear me?' Everyone admits they can hear you blowing. It's only when you speak the microphone goes dead.

Erma Bombeck, *If Life is a Bowl of Cherries – What am I Doing in the Pits?* (1978)

A speech is poetry and cadence, rhythm, imagery, sweep. A speech reminds us that words, like children, have the power to make dance the dullest beanbag of a heart.

Peggy Noonan, *What I Saw at the Revolution* (1990)

And adepts in the speaking trade
Keep a cough by them ready made.

   Charles Churchill, British curate and satirist, *The Ghost*
   (1763)

A heavy and cautious responsibility of speech is the easiest thing in the world: anybody can do it. That is why so many tired, elderly and wealthy men go in for politics.

   G. K. Chesterton, English writer

Desperately accustomed as I am to public speaking...

   Noël Coward, English playwright, opening charity bazaar
   at Oxford

Spontaneous speeches are seldom worth the paper they are written on.

   Leslie Henson, English comedian

The toastmaster introduced the speaker with great fervor, stressing her years of faithful service to the club and eulogizing her ability and charm. Somewhat overwhelmed, the speaker faced the audience. 'After such an introduction,' she said disarmingly, 'I can hardly wait to hear what I've got to say.'

   Adnelle H. Heskett, *Reader's Digest*

I wasn't allowed to speak while my husband was alive, and since he's gone no one has been able to shut me up.

   Hedda Hopper, *From Under Your Hat* (1952)

Why don't th' feller who says, 'I'm not a speechmaker,' let it go at that instead o' givin' a demonstration?

Kin Hubbard, American cartoonist

A toastmaster is a man who eats a meal he doesn't want so he can get up and tell a lot of stories he doesn't remember to people who've already heard them.

George Jessel, industrialist and Justice of the Peace

The human brain starts working the moment you are born and never stops until you stand up to speak in public.

George Jessel, industrialist and Justice of the Peace

When audiences come to see us authors lecture, it is largely in the hope that we'll be funnier to look at than to read.

Sinclair Lewis, American novelist and playwright

A speech is like a love affair. Any fool can start it, but to end it requires considerable skill.

Lord Mancroft, British politician

A speaker who does not strike oil in ten minutes should stop boring.

Louis Nizer, noted American trial lawyer

Speeches are like babies – easy to conceive but hard to deliver.

Pat O'Malley, English singer and actor

He can take a batch of words and scramble them together
and leaven them properly with a hunk of oratory and knock
the White House doorknob right out of a candidate's hand.

Will Rogers, American humorist, on presidential candidate
William Jennings Bryan

I am the most spontaneous speaker in the world because
every word, every gesture, and every retort has been carefully rehearsed.

George Bernard Shaw, Irish playwright

The last time I was in this hall was when my late beloved
boss, Frank Knox, the Secretary of the Navy, spoke here,
and it was a better speech he gave than the one I'll be giving
tonight. I know. I wrote them both.

Adlai Stevenson, American politician

It usually takes me more than three weeks to prepare a
good impromptu speech.

Mark Twain, American author

I like the way you always manage to state the obvious with
a sense of real discovery.

Gore Vidal, *The Best Man* (1960)

Listening to a speech by [Neville] Chamberlain is like
paying a visit to Woolworths – everything in its place and
nothing above sixpence.

Aneurin Bevan, British Labour politician

The most popular speaker is one who sits down before he stands up.

John Pentland Mahaffy, Irish educator and scholar

The best audience is intelligent, well-educated and a little drunk.

Alben W. Barkley, lawyer and Vice-President of the United States 1949–53

Winston [Churchill] has devoted the best years of his life to preparing his impromptu speeches.

F. E. Smith, Conservative statesman and lawyer

The great orator always shows a dash of contempt for the opinions of his audience.

Elbert Hubbard, American writer

I always said Little Truman [Capote] had a voice so high it could only be detected by a bat.

Tennessee Williams, American playwright

It just shows, what any Member of Parliament will tell you, that if you want real oratory, the preliminary noggin is essential. Unless pie-eyed, you cannot hope to grip.

P. G. Wodehouse, *Right Ho, Jeeves* (1934)

Always be shorter than anybody dared to hope.

Lord Reading, Governor-General of India, on speechmaking

Most people tire of a lecture in ten minutes; clever people can do it in five. Sensible people never go to lectures at all. But the people who do go to a lecture and who get tired of it, presently hold it as a sort of grudge against the lecturer personally. In reality his sufferings are worse than theirs.

Stephen Leacock, *My Discovery of England* (1922)

I never lecture, not because I am shy or a bad speaker, but simply because I detest the sort of people who go to lectures and don't want to meet them.

H. L. Mencken, American journalist

Commencement oratory must eschew anything that smacks of partisan politics, political preference, sex, religion or unduly firm opinion. Nonetheless, there must be a speech: Speeches in our culture are the vacuum that fills a vacuum.

John Kenneth Galbraith, Canadian economist

Today's public figures can no longer write their own speeches or books, and there is some evidence that they can't read them either.

Gore Vidal, American writer and political commentator

A speech is a solemn responsibility. The man who makes a bad thirty-minute speech to two hundred people wastes only a half hour of his own time. But he wastes one hundred hours of the audience's time – more than four days – which should be a hanging offense.

Jenkin Lloyd Jones, American newspaper publisher

The ability to speak is a short cut to distinction. It puts a man in the limelight, raises him head and shoulders above the crowd.

Lowell Thomas, American publisher

#STATISTICS

Ninety-seven per cent of all statistics are made up.

Anon.

Say you were standing with one foot in the oven and one foot in an ice bucket. According to the percentage people, you should be perfectly comfortable.

Bobby Bragan, baseball shortstop, catcher, manager and coach

Facts are stubborn things, but statistics are more pliable.

Anon.

Lottery: A tax on people who are bad at maths.

Anon.

He uses statistics as a drunken man uses lampposts – for support rather than for illumination.

Andrew Lang, Scottish poet and critic

Then there was the man who drowned crossing a stream with an average depth of six inches.

Anon.

Somewhere on this globe, every ten seconds, there is a woman giving birth to a child. She must be found and stopped.

Sam Levenson, American humorist

It is now proved beyond a shadow of doubt that smoking is one of the leading causes of statistics.

Fletcher Knebel, American journalist and author

There are two kinds of statistics, the kind you look up and the kind you make up.

Rex Stout, American mystery writer

Get your facts first, then you can distort them as you please.

Mark Twain, American author

I'm right 98 per cent of the time. Who cares about the other 3 per cent?

Facebook, 2012

A statistician is someone who is good with numbers, but lacks the personality to be an accountant.

Anon.

See also #RESEARCH

#STATUS

This is my executive suite and this is my executive vice-president, Ralph Anderson, and my executive secretary,

Adele Eades, and my executive desk and my executive carpet and my executive wastebasket and my executive ashtray and my executive pen set and my ...

Henry Martin, cartoon in the *New Yorker*

#SUCCESS

Sweat is the cologne of accomplishment.

Heywood Hale Broun, American writer

Behind every successful man there stands an amazed woman.

Anon.

I don't think the state does enough for artists and writers generally in the way of subsidy and tax relief and so on. I mean, as an artist and a writer, I have to be surrounded by beautiful things and beautiful people. And beautiful people cost money.

Alan Bennett, 'The Lonely Pursuit', *On the Margin* (1966)

The penalty of success is to be bored by the people who used to snub you.

Nancy Astor, first female British Member of Parliament

It's lonely at the top, but you eat better.

Anon.

It is difficult to make a reputation, but it is even more difficult seriously to mar a reputation once properly made – so faithful is the public.

Arnold Bennett, English novelist

Most of business's great successes are achieved by someone being either clever enough to know it can't be done – or too stupid to realise it can't.

Anon.

If at first you don't succeed, try, try again. Then quit. No use being a damn fool about it.

W. C. Fields, American actor and comedian

Success is all a matter of luck. Ask any failure.

Anon.

If at first you don't succeed, destroy all the evidence that you tried.

Anon.

Success is the one unpardonable sin against our fellows.

Ambrose Bierce, American satirist and critic

You wonder how they do it and you look to see the knack,
You watch the foot in action, or the shoulder, or the back,
But when you spot the answer where the higher glamours lurk,
You'll find in moving higher up the laurel covered spire,
That the most of it is practice and the rest of it is work.

Grantland Rice, sports writer, *How To Be a Champion*

If at first you don't succeed, do it like your mother told you.
  Anon.

There is no point at which you can say, 'Well, I'm successful now. I might as well take a nap.'
  Carrie Fisher, actress and writer

I dread success. To have succeeded is to have finished one's business on earth, like the male spider, who is killed by the female the moment he has succeeded in courtship. I like a state of continual becoming, with a goal in front and not behind.
  George Bernard Shaw, Irish playwright

Success is blocked by concentrating on it and planning for it … Success is shy – it won't come out while you're watching.
  Tennessee Williams, American playwright

It is wise to keep in mind that no success or failure is necessarily final.
  Anon.

I couldn't wait for success – so I went ahead without it.
  Jonathan Winters, American comedian

Nothing succeeds like reputation.
  John Huston, actor

Success didn't spoil me; I've always been insufferable.

Fran Lebowitz, New York columnist

The worst part of having success is to try finding someone who is happy for you.

Bette Midler, actress and singer

It is fatal to be appreciated in one's own time.

Osbert Sitwell, English writer

Failure is very difficult for a writer to bear, but very few can manage the shock of early success.

Maurice Valency, American playwright

The usual drawback to success is that it annoys one's friends so.

P. G. Wodehouse, 'The Man Upstairs' (1914)

The toughest thing about success is that you've got to keep on being a success.

Irving Berlin, American songwriter and lyricist (who kept going until he was 101)

It takes years to make an overnight success.

Eddie Cantor, American performer and comedian

When you struggle hard and lose money you're a hero.
When you start making money, you become a capitalist swine.

Terence Conran, British entrepreneur

I am doomed to an eternity of compulsive work. No set goal achieved satisfies. Success only breeds a new goal. It is endless.

Bette Davis, actress

It's a funny thing about life; if you refuse to accept anything but the best, you very often get it.

Somerset Maugham, English novelist

The truly successful businessman is essentially a dissenter, a rebel who is seldom if ever satisfied with the status quo.

J. Paul Getty, American industrialist

I've always realised that if I'm doing well at business, I'm cutting some other bastard's throat.

Kerry Packer, Australian media magnate

If at first you don't succeed, you may be at your level of incompetence.

Laurence J. Peter, *The Peter Principle*

I shall be like that tree. I shall die at the top.

Jonathan Swift, Anglo-Irish writer

It is not enough to succeed. Others must fail.

Gore Vidal, American writer and political commentator

To achieve great things we must live as though we were never going to die.

Luc de Clapiers Vauvenargues, French soldier and writer

You cannot be a success in any business without believing that it is the greatest business in the world. You have to put your heart in the business and the business in your heart.

Thomas Watson, American founder and president of IBM

Take the obvious, add a cupful of brains, a generous pinch of imagination, a bucketful of courage and daring, stir well and bring to a boil.

Bernard Baruch, American financier and statesman, on enterprise

Think of yourself as on the threshold of unparalleled success. A whole clear, glorious life lies before you. Achieve! Achieve!

Andrew Carnegie, Scottish-American industrialist

The mode by which the inevitable comes to pass, is effort.

Oliver Wendell Holmes, American physician and poet

I've always admired the ability to bite off more than one can chew.
And then chew it.

Thomas Melville, American sailor

The rung of a ladder was never meant to rest upon, but only to hold a man's foot long enough to enable him to put the other somewhat higher.

T. H. Huxley, English biologist

There's a man in the world who is never turned down,
Wherever he chances to stray.
He gets the glad hand in the populous town,
Or out where the farmers make hay.
He's greeted with pleasure on deserts of sand,
Or deep in the aisles of the woods.
Wherever he goes there's a welcoming hand –
He's the man who delivers the goods.

Walt Whitman, American poet

All you need in this life is ignorance and confidence, and then success is sure.

Mark Twain, American author

I'm against a homogenised society because I want the cream to rise.

Robert Frost, American poet

There is only one success – to be able to spend your life in your own way.

Christopher Morley, American writer

Success is never final.

Winston Churchill, British statesman and orator

See also #FAILURE, #SUCCESS AND FAILURE

#SUCCESS AND FAILURE

Being No. 2 sucks.
>Andre Agassi, American tennis player

It's not enough that we succeed. Cats must also fail.
(One dog to another in a bar.)
>Leo Cullum, *New Yorker* (1997)

Failure is the condiment that gives success its flavour.
>Truman Capote, American author

Her failure was a useful preliminary to success.
>Edith Wharton, *The Custom of the Country* (1913)

You always pass failure on your way to success.
>Mickey Rooney, American actor

In Italy for thirty years under the Borgias they had warfare, terror, murder, bloodshed – they produced Michelangelo, Leonardo da Vinci, and the Renaissance. In Switzerland they had brotherly love, five hundred years of democracy and peace, and what did they produce? – the cuckoo clock.
>Graham Greene and Orson Welles, *The Third Man* (1949)

The two hardest things to handle in life are failure and success.
>Anon.

Nothing recedes like success.
>Walter Winchell, American newspaper columnist

Success is going from failure to failure without loss of enthusiasm.

Winston Churchill, British statesman and orator

The Life of Abraham Lincoln

He failed in business in 1831.

He was defeated for Legislature in 1832.

His second failure in business was in 1833.

He suffered a nervous breakdown in 1836.

He was defeated for Speaker in 1838.

He was defeated for Elector in 1840.

He was defeated for Congress in 1843.

Again, he was defeated for Congress in 1848.

He was defeated for Senate in 1855.

He was defeated for Vice President in 1856.

He was defeated for Senate in 1858.

He was elected as President in 1860.

If at first you don't succeed...

Anon.

I don't know the key to success, but the key to failure is trying to please everybody.

Bill Cosby, American comedian and actor

#SUCCESS, SECRETS OF

The sun has not caught me in bed in fifty years.

Thomas Jefferson, Founding Father and President of the United States 1801–09

Few people do business well who do nothing else.

 Philip Dormer Stanhope, 4th Earl of Chesterfield, English
 statesman

The secret of success is to offend the greatest number of people.

 George Bernard Shaw, Irish playwright

I have learned a long time ago not to flinch when someone says they are going to hit you.

 David M. Roderick, American businessman

I not only use all the brains I have but all I can borrow.

 Woodrow Wilson, President of the United States 1913–21

The secret of success is constancy to purpose.

 Benjamin Disraeli, two-time British Prime Minister

If A is success in life, then A equals X plus Y plus Z.
Work is X; Y is play; and Z is keeping your mouth shut.

 Albert Einstein, German theoretical physicist

People who are successful simply want it more than people who are not.

 Ian Shrager, American entrepreneur

Success is a science; if you have the conditions, you get the result.

 Oscar Wilde, Irish playwright

You must do the thing you think you cannot do.

 Eleanor Roosevelt, First Lady of the United States 1933–45

The recipe for success combines two ingredients, luck and pluck. The luck in finding someone to pluck.

Anon.

Success is 10 per cent inspiration, 90 per cent last-minute changes.

Anon.

Seventy per cent of success in life is showing up.

Woody Allen, actor and writer

There's no secret about success. Did you ever know a successful man that didn't tell you all about it.

Kin Hubbard, *Abe Martin's Primer* (1914)

T

#TAXATION

I believe we should all pay our tax bill with a smile. I tried
– but they wanted cash.

Anon.

I've saved enough money to pay my income tax. Now all I
have to do is borrow some to live on.

Lou Costello, American actor and comic

A government that robs Peter to pay Paul can always
depend on the support of Paul.

George Bernard Shaw, Irish playwright

If you make any money, the government shoves you in the
creek once a year with it in your pockets, and all that don't
get wet you can keep.

Will Rogers, American humorist

When there's a single thief, it's robbery. When there are a thousand thieves, it's taxation.

Vanya Cohen, American tax expert

Taxation *with* representation ain't so hot either.

Gerald Barzan, American wit

The art of taxation consists in so plucking the goose as to get the most feathers with the least hissing.

Jean-Baptiste Colbert, French Minister of Finances
1665–83

Unquestionably, there is progress. The average American now pays out twice as much in taxes as he formerly got in wages.

H. L. Mencken, American journalist

Did you ever notice that when you put the words 'The' and 'IRS' together, it spells 'THEIRS'?

Anon.

It's income tax time again, Americans: time to gather up those receipts, get out those tax forms, sharpen up that pencil, and stab yourself in the aorta.

Dave Barry, American author and columnist

You don't pay taxes – they *take* taxes.

Chris Rock, *Bigger and Blacker* (1999)

Why does a slight tax increase cost you two hundred dollars and a substantial tax cut save you thirty cents?

Peg Bracken, American humorist

Any reasonable system of taxation should be based on the slogan of 'Soak the Rich'.

Heywood Broun, American journalist

The only way to cut government spending is not to give them the money to spend in the first place.

Howard Jarvis, publisher and political activist

I told the Inland Revenue I didn't owe them a penny because I live near the seaside.

Ken Dodd, English comedian

I have always paid income tax. I object only when it reaches a stage when I am threatened with having nothing left for my old age – which is due to start next Tuesday or Wednesday.

Noël Coward, English playwright

The income tax has made more liars out of the American people than golf has.

Will Rogers, American humorist

Ask not what your country can do for you, but how much it's going to cost you for them to do it.

Anon.

The rich aren't like us; they pay less taxes.

Peter de Vries, American novelist

If you ask the Inland Revenue, this country is a land of untold wealth.

Sally Poplin, British humorous writer

I'm spending a year dead for tax reasons.

Douglas Adams, British comedy writer

It's getting harder and harder to support the government in the style to which it has become accustomed.

Anon.

It's ridiculous! The average citizen works six months a year for the government. Government *employees* don't work six months a year for the government!

Max Kauffmann, American comedian

People who complain about paying their income tax can be divided into two types: men and women.

Anon.

Taxation: the process by which money is collected from the people in order to pay the salaries of the people who do the collecting.

Freddie Oliver, English comedian

The Eiffel Tower is the Empire State Building after taxes.

Anon.

The Lord giveth and the Inland Revenue taketh away.

Sally Poplin, British humorous writer

The reason the government is worried about lowering taxes is that it might establish a dangerous precedent: the right of people to keep their own money.

Freddie Oliver, English comedian

You've got to hand it to the tax collector. If you don't, he'll come and get it.

Anon.

Taxation without representation may have been tyranny – but it was definitely a lot cheaper.

Max Kauffmann, American comedian

A communist government won't let you make much money. A capitalist government lets you make as much money as you like – they just won't let you keep it.

Max Kauffmann, American comedian

I'm proud to be paying taxes in the United States. The only thing is, I could be just as proud for half the money.

Arthur Godfrey, radio and television broadcaster and entertainer

I used to say I was making a speech on the Senate floor and I said, 'Now, gentlemen, let me tax your memories,' and Kennedy jumped up and said, 'Why haven't we thought of that before?'

Bob Dole, American politician

It's true that nothing is certain except death and taxes. Sometimes I wish they came in that order.

Sam Levenson, American humorist

The taxpayer – that's someone who works for the federal government but doesn't have to take the civil servant examination.

Ronald Reagan, President of the United States 1981–89

Income tax returns are the most imaginative fiction being written today.

Herman Wouk, American novelist

The income tax people are very nice. They're letting me keep my own mother.

Henny Youngman, American comedian

#TEAMWORK

No one can whistle a symphony. It takes a whole orchestra to play it.

H. E. Luccock, theological academic

None of us is as smart as all of us.

Ken Blanchard, author and management guru

Teamwork is essential – it allows you to blame someone else.

Anon.

No matter how much teamwork achieves, the result will be identified with a single name in years to come.

Anon.

A team is a mutual protection society formed to guarantee that no one person can be to blame for a botched committee job that one man would have performed satisfactorily.

Russell Baker, humorous columnist

If you can't feed a team with two large pizzas, it's too large.

Jeff Bezos, Amazon boss

No member of a crew is praised for the rugged individuality of his rowing.

Ralph Waldo Emerson, American essayist and poet

The team effort is a lot of people doing what I say.

Michael Winner, film producer and director

Sure there's no 'I' in 'team,' but there is a 'ME'!

Anon.

#TECHNOLOGY

The typewriting machine, when played with expression, is no more annoying than the piano when played by a sister or near relation.

Oscar Wilde, Irish playwright

All of the biggest technological inventions created by man –
the airplane, the automobile, the computer – say little about
his intelligence, but speak volumes about his laziness.

Mark Kennedy, American politician

Do you realise if it weren't for Edison we'd be watching TV
by candlelight?

Al Boliska, comedian

It is only when they go wrong that machines remind you
how powerful they are.

Clive James, Australian poet and critic

At a recent computer expo (COMDEX), Bill Gates report-
edly compared the computer industry with the auto industry and stated, 'If GM had kept up with technology like the
computer industry has, we would all be driving $25.00 cars
that got 1,000 miles to the gallon.'

In response to Bill's comments, General Motors issued a
press release stating: If GM had developed technology like
Microsoft, we would all be driving cars with the following
characteristics:

1. For no reason whatsoever, your car would crash twice
    a day.
2. Every time they repainted the lines in the road, you
    would have to buy a new car.
3. Occasionally your car would die on the freeway for no
    reason. You would have to pull to the side of the road,
    close all of the windows, shut off the car, restart it, and
    reopen the windows before you could continue.

    For some reason you would simply accept this.

4. Occasionally, executing a maneuver such as a left turn would cause your car to shut down and refuse to restart, in which case you would have to reinstall the engine.

5. Macintosh would make a car that was powered by the sun, was reliable, five times as fast and twice as easy to drive – but would run on only 5 per cent of the roads.

6. The oil, water temperature, and alternator warning lights would all be replaced by a single 'This Car Has Performed An Illegal Operation' warning light.

7. The airbag system would ask 'Are you sure?' before deploying.

8. Occasionally, for no reason whatsoever, your car would lock you out and refuse to let you in until you simultaneously lifted the door handle, turned the key and grabbed hold of the radio antenna.

9. Every time a new car was introduced car buyers would have to learn how to drive all over again because none of the controls would operate in the same manner as the old car.

10. You'd have to press the 'Start' button to turn the engine off.

If the automobile had followed the same development cycle as the computer, a Rolls-Royce would today cost $100, get a million miles per gallon, and explode once a year, killing everyone inside.

Robert X. Cringely, pen name of technology journalists

#TELEPHONES

Telephone, *n.* An invention of the devil which abrogates some of the advantages of making a disagreeable person keep his distance.

Ambrose Bierce, *The Devil's Dictionary* (1911)

The bathtub was invented in 1850 and the telephone in 1875. In other words, if you had been living in 1850, you could have sat in the bathtub for twenty-five years without having to answer the phone.

Bill DeWitt, Major League Baseball executive

The telephone is a good way to talk to people without having to offer them a drink.

Fran Lebowitz, New York columnist

It is my heart-warmed and world-embracing Christmas hope and aspiration that all of us, the high, the low, the rich, the poor, the admired, the despised, the loved, the hated, the civilized, the savage (every man and brother of us all throughout the whole earth), may eventually be gathered together in a heaven of everlasting rest and peace and bliss, except the inventor of the telephone.

Mark Twain, American author

Anybody have plans to stare at their phone somewhere exciting this weekend?

Tumblr, 2012

She texted me: 'Your adorable.' I replied: 'No, YOU'RE adorable.' Now she likes me, but all I did was point out her typo.

Anon.

If The Phone Doesn't Ring, It's Me.

Jimmy Buffett & the Coral Reefer Band, 1985

If people winked in real life as much as they do in texts, the world would be a really creepy place.

Facebook, 2010

A man telephoned a friend at two o'clock in the morning. 'I do hope I haven't disturbed you,' he said.

'Don't worry,' the friend replied, 'I had to get up anyway to answer the phone.'

Anon.

They [wives] are people who think when the telephone bell rings, it is against the law not to answer it.

Ring Lardner, *Say It with Oil* (1923)

Eric: Hey, answer the phone! Answer the phone!
Ernie: But it's not ringing!
Eric: Why leave everything till the last minute?

Eric Morecambe and Ernie Wise, *The Morecambe and Wise Joke Book* (1979)

Public telephones in Europe are like our pinball machines. They are primarily a form of entertainment and a test of skill rather than a means of communication.

Miss Piggy, *Miss Piggy's Guide to Life, As Told to Henry Beard* (1981)

I rang up my local swimming pool and I said, 'Is that the local swimming pool?'
And they said, 'It depends where you're calling from.'

Tommy Cooper, English comedian

No, this is not the Jones's house. You must have a wrong number.
Are you sure?
Have I ever lied to you before?

Tommy Cooper, English comedian

The marvellous thing about mobile phones is that, wherever you are, whatever you are doing, you can keep them switched off so no one will bother you.

Guy Browning, British humorist

There's a new telephone service that lets you test your IQ over the phone. It costs $3.95 a minute. If you make the call at all, you're a moron. If you're on the line for three minutes, you're a complete idiot.

Jay Leno, American television host

See also #SMARTPHONES

#TIME

Time is what prevents everything from happening at once.
John Archibald Wheeler, American theoretical physicist

For disappearing acts, it's hard to beat what happens to the eight hours supposedly left after eight of sleep and eight of work.
Doug Larson, American columnist and editor

A good holiday is one spent among people whose notions of time are vaguer than yours.
J. B. Priestley, English novelist, playwright and broadcaster

If you want work well done, select a busy man – the other kind has no time.
Elbert Hubbard, American writer

Time is an equal opportunity employer. Each human being has exactly the same number of hours and minutes every day. Rich people can't buy more hours. Scientists can't invent new minutes. And you can't save time to spend it on another day. Even so, time is amazingly fair and forgiving. No matter how much time you've wasted in the past, you still have an entire tomorrow.
Denis Waitley, American writer and consultant

Day, *n.* A period of twenty-four hours, mostly misspent.
Ambrose Bierce, *The Devil's Dictionary* (1911)

In bed, its 6 a.m., you close your eyes for five minutes, its 7.45. At school, its 1.30, you close your eyes for five minutes, its 1.31.

Anon.

All it takes is twenty seconds of insane courage to change your life.

Benjamin Mee, British actor, writer and zoologist

#TRADE UNIONS

Mrs Wicksteed: I'm going to my cake-decorating class. I don't really want to, but we're electing a new secretary and it's like everything else: if the rank and file don't go, the militants take over.

Alan Bennett, *Habeas Corpus* (1973)

Unions run by workers are like alcoholic homes run by alcoholics, a sure recipe for tyranny.

Roy Kerridge, *The Lone Conformist* (1984)

Unionism seldom, if ever, uses such power as it has to insure better work; almost always it devotes a large part of that power to safeguarding bad work.

H. L. Mencken, American journalist

Both management and unions agree that time is money. They just can't agree on how much!

Anon.

I'd support any strike for shorter hours. I think sixty minutes is far too long.

Anon.

My dad was a trade unionist. He used to begin our bedtime stories with, 'Once upon a time and a half...'

Anon.

The management were going to cut wages by £50 a week, but don't worry, I've got it backdated to 1 January.

Jerry Dennis, British comedian

Boss: Why are you people always at my throat?
Shop steward: Because it keeps us away from the area you expect us to kiss!

Anon.

First trade unionist: I see the daffodils are out.
Second trade unionist: How does that affect us?

Anon.

A shop steward was telling a meeting of his members that the management had agreed to all their demands.
'From now on, all wages are doubled, holidays are increased to ten weeks per annum and we only have to work on Fridays.'
And a man from the back shouted, 'Not *every* bloody Friday?'

Jerry Dennis, British comedian

Dear Sir,

If we are to stop the militant minorities from taking over our trade unions, we ordinary members have got to be prepared to stand up and be counted.

Yours faithfully, A. N. Other.

Minister of Labor: ... the workers of Freedonia are demanding shorter hours.
Firefly [Groucho Marx]: Very well, we'll give them shorter hours. We'll start by cutting their lunch hour to twenty minutes.

Arthur Sheekman and Nat Perrin, *Duck Soup* (1933)

See also #SOCIALISM

#TWITTER, FACEBOOK AND SOCIAL MEDIA

Oprah: HI TWITTERS, THANK YOU FOR A WARM WELCOME. FEELING REALLY 21ST CENTURY
THE_REAL_SHAQ: @oprah: ur caps r on, btw

Pioneering Twitter exchange, 2009

YOU ARE NOT A GAME OF THRONES CHARACTER. YOU WORK IN AN OFFICE. THE YEAR IS 2013. PLEASE RETURN TO YOUR SPREADSHEET.

Twitter, 2013

The first 1,987,876 people to retweet this will be our official favourite people on Twitter.

Twitter, 2013

Average conversion rates are meaningless. Switzerland on average is flat.

  Twitter, 2012

If you haven't got anything interesting to say, post it on Facebook.

  Twitter

I didn't get any qualifications from school and look at me … I'M ON TWITTER!

  Martin Carr, member of The Boo Radleys

Seeing Linkedin Park tonight. They're like Linkin Park except they don't know who the other band members are or why they're in the band.

  Michael Spicer, British comedian

The way I now consume news: a) See jokes about a story on Twitter b) Try to work out what the story is c) Find story d) Understand jokes.

  Rhodri Marsden, British writer

Twitter is like a bar, Facebook is your living room and LinkedIn is the local chamber of commerce.

  Brenda S. Stoltz, American businesswoman

You are what you tweet.

  Alex Tew, British entrepreneur

The Pope is hardly the first person to lose interest in their real job so soon after joining Twitter.

Twitter, 2013

Every time I almost think humanity is going to be okay, I catch a glimpse of Yahoo Answers.

Facebook, 2013

Ten years from now, one of the hardest challenges our kids will face will be finding a username that's still available.

Facebook, 2012

The best way to engage honestly with the marketplace via Twitter is to never use the words 'engage', 'honestly', or 'marketplace'.

Jeffrey Zeldman, American entrepreneur

LinkedIn is for the people you know. Facebook is for the people you used to know. Twitter is for people you want to know.

Anon.

Our head of social media is the customer.

McDonald's

Twitter provides us with a wonderful platform to discuss/confront societal problems. We trend Justin Bieber instead.

Lauren Leto, creator and writer of *Texts From Last Night*

You can buy attention (advertising). You can beg for attention from the media (PR). You can bug people one at a time to get attention (sales). Or you can earn attention by creating something interesting and valuable and then publishing it online for free.

David Meerman Scott, author and speaker

When you've got five minutes to fill, Twitter is a great way to fill thirty-five minutes.

Twitter, 2011

Twitter is not a technology. It's a conversation. And it's happening with or without you.

Twitter, 2011

How can you squander even one more day not taking advantage of the greatest shifts of our generation? How dare you settle for less when the world has made it so easy for you to be remarkable?

Seth Godin, American marketing guru

See also #COMPUTERS, #INTERNET

U

#UNEMPLOYMENT

The government has discovered a great new way of cutting down on unemployment – they're going to raise the school leaving age to forty-seven.

Jerry Dennis, British comedian

I lost my job. No, I didn't really *lose* my job. I know where my job is, still. It's just that when I go there, there's this new guy doing it.

Bobcat Goldthwait, American comedian

I prefer to think of myself as a freelancer instead of unemployed.

Facebook, 2012

You know you're out of power when your limousine is yellow and your driver speaks Farsi.

James Baker, United States Secretary of State 1989–92

It's no use saying the Labour government works if one and a half million do not.

Joe Haines, British journalist

There comes a time in every man's life when he must make way for an older man.

Reginald Maudling, on being dropped from Mrs Thatcher's shadow Cabinet in 1976

My brother-in-law … I wish he would learn a trade, so we'd know what kind of work he was out of.

Henny Youngman, American comedian

On the plus side, the good thing about unemployment is that it certainly takes the worry out of being late for work.

Anon.

Unemployment is capitalism's way of getting you to plant a garden.

Orson Scott Card, American novelist

The trouble with unemployment is that the minute you wake up in the morning you're on the job.

Slappy White, American comedian

The hardest work in the world is being out of work.

Whitney Young, Jr, American civil rights leader

The government has announced radical new plans to cut the length of the dole queues. They're going to get people to stand closer together.

Jerry Dennis, British comedian

Things are so shaky at work, they hand out your calendar one day at a time.

Anon.

See also #HUMAN RESOURCES

W

#WAGES

We're over-paying him, but he's worth it.
   Sam Goldwyn, Hollywood producer, of actor

Pay your people the least possible and you'll get from them the same.
   Malcolm S. Forbes, American publisher

#WEALTH

I never wanted to be a millionaire. I just wanted to live like one.
   Walter Hagen, American golfer

If you can actually count your money, then you're not rich.
   J. Paul Getty, American industrialist

A man who has a million dollars is as well off as if he were rich.

John Jacob Astor, American industrialist and philanthropist

Wealth – any income that is at least one hundred dollars more a year than the income of one's wife's sister's husband.

H. L. Mencken, American journalist

Wealth is not an end of life, but an instrument of life.

Henry Ward Beecher, American clergyman and social reformer

Nothing is more admirable than the fortitude with which millionaires tolerate the disadvantages of their wealth.

Rex Stout, American detective fiction writer

There are few things in the world more reassuring than an unhappy lottery winner.

Tony Parsons, English novelist

I don't know much about being a millionaire but I'll bet I'd be darling at it.

Dorothy Parker, American wit

The most popular labor-saving device is still money.

Phyllis George, American businesswoman

In every well-governed state, wealth is a sacred thing; in democracies it is the only sacred thing.

Anatole France, French poet and novelist

Those who condemn wealth are those who have none and see no chance of getting it.

William Penn Patrick, American entrepreneur

It is in the interest of the commercial world that wealth should be found everywhere.

Edmund Burke, Irish statesman and philosopher

As a friend of mine once said, 'I don't knock the rich – I've never got a job yet from a poor person.'

Anon.

God shows his contempt for wealth by the kind of person he selects to receive it.

Austin O'Malley, author

Lord Finchley tried to mend the 'lectric light
Himself; it struck him dead: and serve him right!
It is the business of the wealthy man
To give employment to the artisan.

Hilaire Belloc, Anglo-French writer

Down with the idle rich!
The bloated upper classes.
They drive to Lord's
In expensive Fords
With their jewelled op'ra glasses.

Noël Coward, 'Down with the Whole Damn Lot!' (1928)

Wealth is not without its advantages, and the case to the contrary, although it has often been made, has never proved widely persuasive.

John Kenneth Galbraith, *The Affluent Society* (1958)

Nouveau is better than no riche at all.

Monsieur Marc (Marc deCoster), New York society hairdresser

The only reason to have money is to tell any sonavabitch in the world to go to hell.

Humphrey Bogart, American actor

Nothing so gives the illusion of intelligence as personal association with large sums of money.

John Kenneth Galbraith, Canadian economist

Cary Grant is so rich, he could, if he wanted, join NATO.

Time magazine

The greatest luxury of riches is that they allow you to escape so much good advice.

Arthur Helps, English writer and Dean of the Privy Council

A fool and his money are soon married.

Carolyn Wells, American author and poet

The man who dies rich, dies disgraced.

Andrew Carnegie, Scottish-American industrialist

Having money is rather like being a blonde. It is more fun but not vital.

    Mary Quant, British fashion designer

I am rich beyond the dreams of avarice.

    Edward Moore, *The Gamester* (1753)

Wealth is like sea water: the more we drink, the thirstier we become; the same is true of fame.

    Arthur Schopenhauer, German philosopher

I am a Millionaire. That is my religion.

    George Bernard Shaw, *Major Barbara* (1907)

He's so rich …
… he's got a walk-in wallet.
… he spends the summer in a little place he's just bought up
    north. It's called Canada.
… he even got a boy for his dog.
… he goes to drive-in movies in a taxi.
… whenever he cashed a cheque, the bank bounced.
… Barclays Bank opened a branch in his living room.
… even his chauffeur has a chauffeur.
… he used to give away his new Mercedes when the ashtrays
    got full.
… he has two swimming pools – one for rinsing.
… he has four cars – one for each direction.
… he has two nose specialists – one for each nostril!
… he has Perrier on the knee!

    Jerry Dennis, British comedian

People's wealth and worth are very rarely related.
   Malcolm S. Forbes, American publisher

I don't like money actually, but it quiets my nerves.
   Joe Louis, American heavyweight boxer

Another advantage of being rich is that all your faults are called eccentricities.
   Anon.

I'd like to be rich enough so that I could throw soap away after the letters are worn off.
   Andy Rooney, American television commentator

#WEALTH – THE DEBIT SIDE

She had so many gold teeth she used to sleep with her head in a safe.
   W. C. Fields, American actor and comedian

Some people get so rich they lose all respect for humanity. That's how rich I want to be.
   Rita Rudner, American comedian

It is the wretchedness of being rich that you have to live with rich people.
   Logan Pearsall Smith, American essayist and critic

The rich man and his daughter are soon parted.
   Kin Hubbard, American cartoonist

The rich are the scum of the earth in every country.
    G. K. Chesterton, *The Flying Inn* (1912)

The more money an American accumulates, the less interesting he becomes.
    Gore Vidal, American writer and political commentator

The prosperous man is never sure that he is loved for himself.
    Lucan (Marcus Annaeus Lucanus), Roman poet

If you pick up a starving dog and make him prosperous, he will not bite you. This is the principal difference between a dog and a man.
    Mark Twain, American author

Rich men feel misfortunes that fly over poor men's heads.
    Anon.

No Rockefeller on the record is ever known to have had a good time.
    Lucius Beebe, American author

Since I am known as a 'rich' person, I feel I have to tip at least $5 each time I check my coat. On top of that, I would have to wear a very expensive coat and it would have to be insured. Added up, without a topcoat, I save over $20,000 each year.
    Aristotle Onassis, Greek shipping magnate

A fortune is usually the greatest misfortune to children. It takes the muscles out of the limbs, the brain out of the head and the virtue out of the heart.

Henry Ward Beecher, American clergyman and social reformer

#WEEKENDS

There aren't enough days in the weekend.

Rod Schmidt, American comedian

Weekends are a bit like rainbows; they look good from a distance but disappear when you get up close to them.

John Shirley, American science-fiction writer

Weekends don't count unless you spend them doing something completely pointless.

Bill Watterson, American author and artist

Nothing ruins a Friday like realising it's only Wednesday.

Pinterest, 2014

The only reason why we ask other people how their weekend was is so we can tell them about our own weekend.

Chuck Palahniuk, American author and journalist

Every man has a right to a Saturday-night bath.

Lyndon B. Johnson, President of the United States 1963–69

Always strive to excel, but only on weekends.
  Richard Rorty, American philosopher

Give a man a fish and he has food for a day; teach him how to fish and you can get rid of him for the entire weekend.
  Zenna Scha, American author

There is little chance that meteorologists can solve the mysteries of weather until they gain an understanding of the mutual attraction of rain and weekends.
  Arnot Sheppard, American wit

#WINNERS AND LOSERS

He who owns the most when he dies, wins.
  Ivan Boesky, American financier

No one remembers who came second.
  Walter Hagen, American golfer

Winning is everything. The only ones who remember you when you come second are your wife and your dog.
  Damon Hill, British Formula One racing driver

Winning is like shaving – you do it every day or you wind up looking like a bum.
  Jack Kemp, American politician and former football player

Whoever said 'It's not whether you win or lose that counts' probably lost.

> Martina Navratilova, Czech-American tennis player

I think I fail a bit less than everyone else.

> Jack Nicklaus, golfer, when asked about the secret of his success

The winner is simply someone who gets up one more time than they fall over.

> Robin Sieger, British businessman and author

The problem with the rat race is that even if you win, you're still a rat.

> Lily Tomlin, American comedian

It matters not whether you win or lose; what matters is whether *I* win or lose.

> Darrin Weinberg, American wit

See also #SUCCESS

#WOMEN

There is a special place in hell for women who do not help other women.

> Madeleine Albright, first female United States Secretary of State 1997–2001

The economic victims of the era are men who know some-one has made off with their future – and they suspect the thief is a woman.

Anon.

Women get the last word in every argument. Anything a man says after that is the beginning of a new argument.

Anon.

Women really do rule the world. They just haven't figured it out yet. When they do, and they will, we're all in big, big trouble.

Anon.

Until Eve arrived, this was a man's world.

Richard Armour, American artist

No man naturally can imagine any more compelling busi-ness for a woman than being interested in him.

Mary Austin, *A Woman of Genius* (1912)

The thing women have yet to learn is nobody gives you power. You just take it.

Roseanne Barr, American actress and comedian

Life's a bitch and so am I.

Bumper sticker, Santa Monica

Women are the only oppressed group in our society that lives in intimate association with their oppressors.

Evelyn Cunningham, journalist and political aide

Anytime you have a fiercely competitive, change-oriented growth business where results count and merit matters, women will rise to the top.

Carly Fiorina, President and CEO of Hewlett Packard

A woman can say more in a sigh than a man can say in a sermon.

Arnold Haultain, British writer

Women are natural guerrillas. Scheming, we nestle into the enemy's bed, avoiding open warfare, watching the options, playing the odds.

Sally Kempton, American author

Nobody will ever win the Battle of the Sexes. There's just too much fraternising with the enemy.

Henry Kissinger, American diplomat

Women who make men talk better than they are accustomed to are always popular.

E. V. Lucas, English writer and assistant editor of *Punch*

Most hierarchies were established by men who now monopolise the upper levels, thus depriving women of opportunities for incompetence.

Laurence J. Peter, American wit

If a man mulls over a decision, they say, 'He's weighing the options.' If a woman does it, they say, 'She can't make up her mind.'

Barbara Proctor, American advertising executive

A man can sleep around, no questions asked, but if a woman makes nineteen or twenty mistakes, she's a tramp.

Joan Rivers, American comedian

Whatever women do they must do twice as well as men to be thought half as good. Luckily, this is not difficult.

Charlotte Whitton, English writer

How to Tell a Businessman from a Businesswoman

- A businessman is aggressive; a businesswoman is pushy.
- He is good on details; she is picky.
- He loses his temper because he's so involved in his job; she is bitchy.
- When he is depressed (or hungover), everyone tiptoes past his office; she is moody, so it must be her time of the month.
- He follows through; she doesn't know when to quit.
- He's confident; she's conceited.
- He stands firm; she's impossible to deal with.
- He is firm; she is hard.
- His judgments are her prejudices.
- He drinks because of the excessive job pressure; she's a lush.
- He isn't afraid to say what he thinks; she's mouthy.
- He's close-mouthed; she's secretive.
- He climbed the ladder to success; she slept her way to the top.
- He is a stern taskmaster; she's hard to work for.
- He is witty; she is sarcastic.

Today's Woman

The two women exchanged the kind of glance women use when no knife is handy.

Ellery Queen, fictional mystery writer and amateur detective

I'd much rather be a woman than a man. Women can cry, they can wear cute clothes, and they're the first to be rescued off sinking ships.

Gilda Radner, American comedian

I would rather trust a woman's instinct than a man's reason.

Stanley Baldwin, three-time British Prime Minister

You should never say anything to a woman that even remotely suggests that you think she's pregnant unless you can see an actual baby emerging from her at that moment.

Dave Barry, *Things That It Took Me 50 Years to Learn* (2007)

I am woman! I am invincible! I am pooped!

T-shirt, New York

Brains are an asset, if you hide them.

Mae West, American actress and wit

The people I'm furious with are the women's liberationists. They keep getting up on soapboxes and proclaiming women are brighter than men. That's true, but it should be kept quiet or it ruins the whole racket.

Anita Loos, American screenwriter and author

The test for whether or not you can hold a job should not be the arrangement of your chromosomes.

Bella Abzug, feminist author and campaigner

I refuse to believe that trading recipes is silly. Tunafish casserole is at least as real as corporate stock.

Barbara Grizzuti Harrison, American journalist

Some of us are becoming the men we wanted to marry.

Gloria Steinem, American journalist and feminist activist

Several men I can think of are as capable, as smart, as funny, as compassionate, and as confused – as remarkable you might say – as most women.

Jane Howard, American journalist and writer

Sometimes the best man for the job isn't.

Anon.

It starts when you sink in his arms and ends with your arms in his sink.

Anon.

During the feminist revolution, the battle lines were again simple. It was easy to tell the enemy, he was the one with the penis. This is no longer strictly true. Some men are okay now. We're allowed to like them again. We still have to keep them in line, of course, but we no longer have to shoot them on sight.

Cynthia Heimel, *Sex Tips for Girls* (1983)

Women are not the weak, frail little flowers that they are advertised. There has never been anything invented yet, including war, that a man would enter into, that a woman wouldn't, too.

Will Rogers, American humorist

One does not have to sleep with, or even touch, someone who has paid for your meal. All those obligations are hereby rendered null and void, and any man who doesn't think so needs a quick jab in the kidney.

Cynthia Heimel, *Sex Tips for Girls* (1983)

Remember, no one can make you feel inferior without your consent.

Eleanor Roosevelt, First Lady of the United States 1933–45

Men are made to be managed and women are born managers.

George Meredith, *The Ordeal of Richard Feverel* (1859)

Women have no need to prove their manhood.

Wilma Scott Heide, American feminist activist

Top jobs are designed for people with wives.

Lucy Heller, British businesswoman

Men are vain, but they won't mind women working so long as they get smaller salaries for the same job.

Irvin Cobb, American wit

Next Mood Swing: 7 Minutes

T-shirt, Pasadena

It is now possible for a flight attendant to get a pilot pregnant.

Richard J. Ferris, President of United Airlines

A woman is like a tea-bag; you never know how strong she is until she gets in hot water.

Nancy Reagan, First Lady of the United States 1981–89

Does giving birth make me a real woman? No, earning less than a man makes me a real woman.

Suzy Berger, actress and writer

Feminine intuition, a quality perhaps even rarer in women than in men.

Ada Levenson, English novelist

You can have it all. You just can't have it all at once.

Oprah Winfrey, American television host

A man at a desk in a room with a closed door is a man at work. A woman at a desk in any room is available.

Marya Mannes, American author and critic

The way to fight a woman is with your hat – grab it and run.

John Barrymore, American actor

The history of women is the history of the worst form of tyranny the world has ever known. The tyranny of the weak over the strong. It is the only tyranny that lasts.

Oscar Wilde, *A Woman of No Importance* (1893)

Nature has given women so much power that the law has very wisely given them little.

Samuel Johnson, English writer

Being powerful is like being a lady. If you have to tell people you are, you aren't.

Margaret Thatcher, British Prime Minister 1979–90

No one should have to dance backward all their lives.

Jill Ruckelshaus, US Commission on Civil Rights

My vigor, vitality and cheek repel me. I am the kind of woman I would run away from.

Nancy Astor, first female British Member of Parliament

Behind almost every woman you ever heard of stands a man who let her down.

Naomi Bliven, American critic

There are three things a woman ought to look – straight as a dart, supple as a snake, and proud as a tiger lily.

Elinor Glyn, *The Sayings of Grandmama and Others* (1908)

The word 'lady': most often used to describe someone you wouldn't want to talk to for even five minutes.

Fran Lebowitz, *Metropolitan Life* (1978)

There is only one political career for which women are perfectly suitable: diplomacy.

Clare Boothe Luce, American editor and activist

Every woman is a rebel, and usually in wild revolt against herself.

Oscar Wilde, *A Woman of No Importance* (1893)

I think women tend to be very hard on themselves and push themselves very hard to get things right. We're bombarded with media images of perfection in every area – thinking we're supposed to be the girl in the 24-hour mascara ad with a bottom like two snooker balls who rushes from the gym to the board meeting and home to a perfect husband and kids, to cook a Michelin-star dinner for twelve people. Life isn't like that. I think maybe it's a relief to see Bridget [Jones] trying to do it and ending up in her underwear with wet hair and one foot in a pan of mashed potato wanting to shout 'Oh go f*** yourselves' at her guests.

Helen Fielding, English novelist

A man without a woman is like a neck without a pain.

Graffito, Los Angeles

I remembered Cliff Wainwright saying once that women were like the Russians – if you did exactly what they wanted all the time you were being realistic and constructive and promoting the cause of peace, and if you ever stood up to them you were resorting to cold-war tactics and pursuing imperialistic designs and interfering in their internal affairs. And by the way of course peace was more peaceful, but if you went on promoting its cause long enough you ended up Finlandised at best.

Kingsley Amis, *Stanley and the Women* (1984)

... this may sound ridiculous, but I've never to this day really known what most women think about anything. Completely closed book to me. I mean, God bless them, what would we do without them? But I've never understood them. I mean, damn it all, one minute you're having a perfectly good time and the next you suddenly see them there like – some old sports jacket or something – literally beginning to come apart at the seams.

Alan Ayckbourn, *Absurd Person Singular* (1974)

On one issue at least, men and women agree; they both distrust women.

H. L. Mencken, American journalist

When women kiss, it always reminds one of prize fighters shaking hands.

H. L. Mencken, *Sententiae* (1920)

... why haven't women got labels on their foreheads saying, 'Danger: Government Health Warning: women can seriously damage your brains, genitals, current account, confidence, razor blades and good standing among your friends.'

Jeffrey Bernard, *Spectator* (1984)

One of the functions of women is to bring an element of trouble into the otherwise tranquil lives of men.

Alan Bennett, *The Lady in the Van* (1989)

Women have more imagination than men. They need it to tell us how wonderful we are.

Arnold H. Glasow, American comic writer

Their heads are full of cotton, hay and rags!
  Anon.

After equality, wage parity, liberation of body and soul, and the extension for the ratification of the ERA, women still can't do the following:
- Start barbecue fires.
- Hook up a stereo.
- Shine shoes.
- Anything on a roof.
- Decide where to hang a picture.
- Investigate mysterious house noises at night.
- Kill and dispose of large insects.
- Walk past a mirror without stopping to look.
  P. J. O'Rourke and John Hughes, *National Lampoon*
  (1979)

Women Jokes. It is important to remember when making jokes about women that they are *not* a minority, they *weren't* captured on another continent and brought here in leg-irons (funny shoes, yes, but not leg-irons) and Hitler *didn't* blame them for Germany's loss of World War I. Therefore you can make any kind of fun of them you want.
  P. J. O'Rourke and John Hughes, *National Lampoon*
  (1979)

A woman's place is in the wrong.
  James Thurber, American humorist and cartoonist

I hate women because they always know where things are.
James Thurber, American humorist and cartoonist

If you want something said, ask a man. If you want something done, ask a woman.
Margaret Thatcher, British Prime Minister 1979–90

Women have a wonderful instinct about things. They can discover everything except the obvious.
Oscar Wilde, *An Ideal Husband* (1895)

A good part – and definitely the most fun part – of being a feminist, is about frightening men.
Julie Burchill, British writer

High heels were invented by a woman who had been kissed on the forehead.
Christopher Morley, American writer

Hysteria is a natural phenomenon, the common denominator of the female nature. It's the big female weapon, and the test of a man is his ability to cope with it.
Tennessee Williams, *The Night of the Iguana* (1961)

If a man speaks in the forest and there is no woman around to hear him, is he still wrong?
Jerry Dennis, British comedian

If only women came with pull-down menus and on-line help.
Anon.

Men don't know much about women. We do know when they're happy, we know when they're crying and we know when they're pissed off. We just don't know in what order these are going to come at us.

Evan Davis, American stand-up comic

#WORDS OF WISDOM

There are two essential strategies in business:
1. Never reveal all you know.

Richard Branson, British business magnate

Why join the navy if you can be a pirate?

Steve Jobs, Apple entrepreneur and inventor

Accomplishing the impossible means only that the boss will add it to your regular duties.

Doug Larson, American columnist and editor

If you can't convince them, confuse them.

Harry S. Truman, President of the United States 1945–53

Indecision is the key to flexibility.

Anon.

Life is like a dogsled team. If you ain't the lead dog, the scenery never changes.

Lewis Grizzard, humorist

What the caterpillar perceives as the end, to the butterfly is just a beginning.
  Buddhist proverb

Speak the truth, but leave immediately after.
  Anon.

Make it idiot-proof and someone will make a better idiot.
  Max Kauffmann, American comedian

A clean desk is a sign of a cluttered desk drawer.
  Sally Poplin, British humorous writer

See also #ADVICE, #APHORISMS

#WORK

Hard work never kills anyone who supervises it.
  Harry Bauer, American businessman

Work was like cats were supposed to be; if you disliked and feared it and tried to keep out of its way, it knew at once and sought you out ...
  Kingsley Amis, *Take a Girl Like You* (1960)

Farming looks mighty easy when your plow is a pencil and you're a thousand miles from a cornfield.
  Dwight D. Eisenhower, President of the United States 1953–61

It is necessary to work, if not from inclination, at least from despair. Everything considered, work is less boring than amusing oneself.

Charles Baudelaire, French poet and critic

People love chopping wood. In this activity one immediately sees results.

Albert Einstein, German theoretical physicist

Thank God every morning when you get up, that you have something to do that day which must be done, whether you like it or not. Being forced to work and forced to do your best will breed in you temperance and self-control, diligence and strength of will, cheerfulness and content, and a hundred virtues which the idle never know.

Charles Kingsley, English academic, historian and novelist

They were a people so primitive they did not know how to get money, except by working for it.

Joseph Addison, English writer

If you don't want to work, you have to work to earn enough money so that you won't have to work.

Ogden Nash, American poet

Anyone can do any amount of work, provided it isn't the work he is supposed to be doing at that moment.

Robert Benchley, American wit

Work is much more fun than fun.

Noël Coward, English playwright

If a train station is where the train stops, what's a work station?
  Anon.

We pretend to work because they pretend to pay us.
  Anon.

Many people quit looking for work when they find a job.
  Anon.

Monday is a lame way to spend one-seventh of your life.
  Anon.

I have never liked working. To me a job is an invasion of privacy.
  Danny McGoorty, billiards hustler

Oh, you hate your job? Why didn't you say so? There's a support group for that. It's called *everybody*, and they meet at the bar.
  Drew Carey, American comedian

If you are the boss it's wise to remember that there are lots of things you don't know and lots of people who hope you won't find out.
  Michael Josephson, speaker on ethics

I thought I wanted a career. Turns out I just wanted a paycheck.
  Office poster, Los Angeles

Homer: Listen to me, Mr Bigshot! If you're looking for the kind of employee who takes abuse and never sticks up for himself, I'm your man! You can treat me like dirt and I'll *still* kiss your butt and call it ice cream. And if *you* don't like it, *I* can change!

Mr Burns: I like your attitude – feisty yet spineless! ... Welcome aboard, son!

Jeff Martin, 'I Married Margie', *The Simpsons* (1991)

The longer the title, the less important the job.

George McGovern, historian and presidential nominee

Work is the greatest thing in the world, so we should always save some of it for tomorrow.

Don Herold, humorist and cartoonist

Work is the refuge of people who have nothing better to do.

Oscar Wilde, Irish playwright

There's nothing wrong with work as long as it doesn't take up too much of your spare time.

Anon.

Hard work never hurt anyone who hired somebody else to do it.

Anon.

Work expands so as to fill the time available for its completion.

C. Northcote Parkinson, *Parkinson's Law* (1957)

Wouldn't this be a great world if insecurity and desperation made us more attractive?

James L. Brooks, *Broadcast News* (1987)

Most people work just hard enough not to get fired and get paid just enough money not to quit.

George Carlin, *Brain Droppings* (1997)

People who work sitting down get paid more than people who work standing up.

Ogden Nash, American poet

For this real or imagined overwork there are, broadly speaking, three possible remedies. He (A) may resign; he may ask to halve the work with a colleague called B; he may demand the assistance of two subordinates, to be called C and D. There is probably no instance, however, in history of A choosing any but the third alternative.

C. Northcote Parkinson, *Parkinson's Law* (1957)

One of the symptoms of approaching nervous breakdown is the belief that one's work is terribly important. If I were a medical man, I should prescribe a holiday to any patient who considered his work important.

Bertrand Russell, British philosopher (attrib.)

Work is the curse of the drinking classes.

Oscar Wilde, Irish playwright

See also #LAZINESS

Y

#YOUTH

Youth is a period of missed opportunities.
  Cyril Connolly, English critic

It is not possible for civilisation to flow backwards while there is youth in the world.
  Helen Keller, American author and political activist

When you're green, you're growing.
When you're ripe, you rot.
  Ray Kroc, founder of the Ronald McDonald Foundation

Nothing so dates a man as to decry the younger generation.
  Adlai Stevenson, American politician

For God's sake, give me the young man who has brains enough to make a fool of himself.
  Robert Louis Stevenson, Scottish novelist

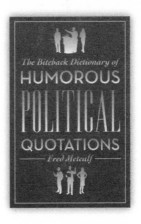

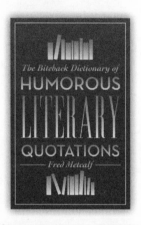

Available now from Biteback Publishing

POLITICAL QUOTATIONS

Available from all good bookshops or order from
www.bitebackpublishing.com